Status Games

Status Games

Why We Play and How to Stop

Loretta Graziano Breuning, PhD
Inner Mammal Institute

ROWMAN &
LITTLEFIELD
Lanham • Boulder • New York • London

ROWMAN &
LITTLEFIELD

An imprint of The Rowman & Littlefield Publishing Group, Inc.
4501 Forbes Blvd., Ste. 200
Lanham, MD 20706
www.rowman.com

Distributed by NATIONAL BOOK NETWORK

British Library Cataloguing in Publication Information available

Library of Congress Cataloging-in-Publication Data

Names: Breuning, Loretta Graziano, author.
Title: Status games : why we play and how to stop / Loretta Graziano
  Breuning, PhD, Inner Mammal Institute.
Description: Lanham, MD : Rowman & Littlefield, [2021] | Includes index. |
  Summary: "People care about status despite their best intentions because
  our brains are wired this way. But playing status games can be
  stressful, anxiety-provoking, and joy-stealing. Learn to rewire your
  brain to replace the trap of social comparison with joy of
  self-confidence" —Provided by publisher.
Identifiers: LCCN 2021010696 (print) | LCCN 2021010697 (ebook) | ISBN
  9781538144190 (pbk. ; alk. paper) | ISBN 9781538144206 (electronic)
Subjects: LCSH: Self-confidence. | Social status. |
  Happiness—Physiological aspects.
Classification: LCC BF575.S39 B75 2021 (print) | LCC BF575.S39 (ebook) |
  DDC 158.1—dc23
LC record available at https://lccn.loc.gov/2021010696
LC ebook record available at https://lccn.loc.gov/2021010697

For my grandson,
Mateo Curbelo

Contents

Preface

How I Stopped Selling

Many years ago, I saw the words "Brand You!" on a magazine cover. The article promised success if you think of yourself as a brand and diligently sell your brand. I hated this idea. My definition of success was being able to stop selling.

I had the same problem with romance. I saw people selling themselves to new partners all the time. My idea of love was being able to stop selling. I did not want the kind of love that requires constant monitoring of the marketplace and supplying what the market demands.

I thought something was wrong with me because of my discomfort with selling. But in time, I realized that everyone hates it. So why does everyone feel pressure to do it? We tend to blame society and our families for this thought loop. We tend to think we can't escape it until we create a utopia where everyone feels valued all the time without having to do anything for it. I searched for that utopia and didn't find it.

But I found something better: the facts about how our brain creates these feelings. In the state of nature, social comparison has life-or-death consequences, so natural selection built a brain that responds to social comparisons with life-or-death brain chemistry. Animals have strong feelings about their social position, and we have inherited the brain system that creates these feelings. I relaxed when I understood the origins of my feelings. You can relax too. Nothing is wrong with us. We're mammals!

You have surely heard of Lake Wobegon, "where all the men are tall, all the women are good looking, and all the children are above average." I grew up in Lake Worseoff, where everyone felt short, ugly, and stupid. I thought the way to be happy was to move to Lake Wobegon. But when I got there, I realized that people are all the same. We all fret over social comparison because we've all inherited a limbic brain that does that. Fortunately, we have power over these emotions when we know how we create them.

Introduction

Why We Care about Status

This book shows how status stimulates the good feeling of serotonin, and how you can enjoy serotonin without endless status games. This is a different way to look at life; but once you know the facts, you will enjoy a new sense of calm. Anyone can do it, in three simple steps:

1. Recognize your mammalian urge for social importance instead of believing what your verbal brain tells you.
2. Replace your old serotonin habit with a new one that puts you up without putting others down.
3. Repeat this new thought loop for six weeks, so the new pathway feels as natural as your old one.

This is hard because the verbal brain doesn't understand the mammal brain it's attached to. Your verbal brain says, "I don't care about status" even as your mammal brain cares with a neurochemical sense of urgency. In the modern world, acknowledging your animal urge for social importance is taboo. It's more socially acceptable to talk about your sex life than to admit that you care about status. But once you get real about your inner mammal, you have power over it.

IT'S NOT EASY BEING MAMMAL

Humans are status conscious because animals are status conscious, and we've inherited the brain structures that motivate them. This may be hard to believe since we're told that animals are cooperative and "our society" causes status seeking. But a close look at the status games of animals reveals patterns we know well from daily life. Mammals strive to one-up each other with all the energy they have left after meeting basic needs. Mammals cooperate when it helps them raise their status, and they compete when that yields more status. They do this because the mammal brain rewards you with a good feeling when you dominate and alarms you with threat chemicals when you submit.

We have inherited this brain chemistry. It gives us life-or-death feelings about status despite our best intentions. When you know how your mammal brain does this, you can enjoy the world as it is instead of feeling threatened by status games. You can't control the world, but you can control your brain more than you realize.

Researchers have studied the status distinctions in mammalian herds and packs and troops for over a century. We know that mammals who raise their status are more able to spread their genes. They don't think consciously about genetics, of course. They just do what feels good, and natural selection built a brain that rewards them with a good feeling (serotonin) when they raise their status. And it alerts them with a bad feeling (cortisol) when they see a threat to their status. Humans have the same chemicals, and we control them with the same brain structures (the amygdala, hippocampus, pituitary, etc., collectively known as the limbic system). So our strong feelings about status are not a mystery.

Humans differ from other animals because of our big cortex, which gives us language and awareness of the future. The animal brain cannot process language or think about the future. This is why the animal brain inside you cannot tell you in words why it feels good or bad, and why it does not care about the future consequences of the things that make you feel good today. Your animal brain just strives to repeat behaviors that trigger happy chemicals and avoid behaviors that trigger unhappy chemicals.

You don't think this consciously, of course. Your limbic brain and your verbal brain are not on speaking terms. This is why you can long for the good feeling of social importance while saying you do not. Status games result.

To make life even harder, serotonin is quickly metabolized. The good feeling soon passes, then you need another moment of social dominance to enjoy more of it. This is why status games are so relentless.

To complicate life further, each brain seeks status in whatever way it got it before. Neurons connect when serotonin flows, which wires us to expect good feelings in the ways we've already experienced them. You seek recognition however you got it in your past. Conscious thought is not involved, because the electricity in your brain flows so easily into the pathways connected by past experience. The recognition you expect does not always come, alas. Disappointment triggers cortisol, which makes you feel like your survival is threatened. You don't think that consciously, but you can end up feeling very threatened in a life that is vastly safer than your ancestors' lives.

We've inherited a brain designed to monitor threats. Neurons connect when cortisol flows, which wires you to scan constantly for whatever made you feel bad in the past. Your threatened feelings are hard for your verbal brain to make sense of. You don't know how you produce them internally, so you see them as evidence of a real external threat. It seems like others are putting you down intentionally because you don't see your own urge to be one-up.

It's not easy being mammal!

WHY YOU PLAY THE GAME

It feels like you don't have a choice. Everyone else seems to be striving for the one-up position, so your inner mammal knows you'll end up in the one-down position if you don't play the game. You want to ignore these thoughts, but neurochemistry is powerful. Status games keep commanding your attention because:

- Cortisol creates a full-body sense of alarm that's designed to get your attention.
- Serotonin is quickly metabolized, so you always have to do more to get more.

- We interpret these impulses as facts about the external world because we don't know how we produce them internally.

Your coworkers are mammals. Your friends and family are mammals. Your beloved is a mammal. You are a mammal too. We all have ups and downs thanks to the brain we've inherited.

Fortunately, you can build new pathways to stimulate serotonin and relieve cortisol in new ways. But it's hard work. It's like learning a foreign language—you have to repeat a new input a lot to build new wiring. You don't remember the repetition that wired in your native language, nor do you remember the repetition that wired in your old status impulses. But you keep using your old wiring unless you build new wiring.

You won't do the work if you blame the external world for your feelings. So let's look closer at status games in animals. You will see patterns that are eerily familiar.

WHY ANIMALS CARE ABOUT STATUS

Mammals live in groups for protection from predators. Each mammal strives to meet its own survival needs because happy chemicals are released when it does that. It's hard to live cheek-by-jowl with critters focused on their own survival, but a mammal who leaves the group is easily picked off by predators. Thus, the ability to coexist was naturally selected. But that doesn't mean a mammal feels good about its group all the time.

We tend to romanticize animal groups instead of seeing the whole story. We imagine animals having the solidarity and mutual support that we long for. But the fact is that animals one-up their group mates when it promotes their own survival. Conflict is avoided because weaker individuals back down to avoid harm. Natural selection built a brain that constantly compares its strength to others. When it sees that it's stronger, it feels safe to act on the urge to meet its needs. When it sees that it's weaker, it feels unsafe and restrains the impulse. This is not what you usually hear about animals, so we must zoom in closer on the drama of nature.

Mammals inherited the brains of reptiles and then added on. Reptiles don't cooperate in their quest to meet their needs. Mammals developed the ability to tolerate and even support others when that promotes the survival of their genes.

Reptiles never seek the company of fellow reptiles. When a reptile sees a smaller individual, it tries to eat it. When it sees a bigger individual, it runs for its life. When it sees a same-size critter, it tries to mate it. (This is less true of birds, which were recently reclassified reptiles.) Fine social distinctions are not made by the reptile brain, yet reptiles have survived for millions of years.

Reptiles survive by making babies in huge numbers, so a species survives even though most babies die. Mammals can't do this because it's harder to gestate a warm-blooded baby. Mammals have so few babies that they must keep more of them alive. They meet this survival challenge by seeking strength in numbers. But it's complicated because each mammal has a survival-seeking reptile brain beneath its support-seeking mammal brain. Each mammal is highly motivated to do what it takes to meet its survival needs. Mammals can only live side by side if they can restrain that impulse.

But they only restrain it when it promotes their survival. The harsh fact of life is that stronger mammals steal food from weaker group mates when that is the better survival choice. If the weaker individual resists, it gets bitten. The pain of a bite wires a brain to fear asserting in the presence of a stronger individual. Juveniles have a grace period, but once juvenile markings fade, a young mammal struggles to fill its belly. A struggle for reproductive opportunity comes after that. Each brain is deciding whether to assert or hold back in each moment.

Navigating this social minefield is the job the mammal brain evolved to do. It releases the stress chemical, cortisol, when it sees itself in the position of weakness. It releases serotonin when it sees itself in the position of strength. *Serotonin is not aggression but a calm confidence in your own strength.* Serotonin creates the feeling that you are safe because you have the capacity to meet your survival needs.

Reptiles are hard-wired at birth, but the mammal brain wires itself from experience. Each serotonin experience wires a young mammal to expect more good feelings from similar situations. Each cortisol surge wires a young brain to expect bad feelings in similar contexts. Thus, without words or curriculum development experts, a young mammal gets wired to do what it takes to keep its genes alive.

For example, a young monkey wakes up hungry each morning and must find food to relieve that internal threat signal. When it sees a piece of fruit, the little monkey surveys the social scene before taking action. If it sees a bigger monkey nearby, it looks elsewhere. When it finds food near a smaller monkey, serotonin is released, and it feels safe to act. It is able to weigh its relative strength thanks to the activity we call "play." If you watch young animals at play, you see that they are quite rough. Each brain wires in expectations about when to expect pain, and when to rejoice in its own strength. At puberty, this same guidance system helps a mammal find reproductive opportunity.

The appetite for social dominance is more primal than the appetite for food and sex because it always comes first.

The point is not that we should bite weaker individuals. The point is that our brain makes social comparisons and reacts with strong feelings. We learn to restrain the impulse to grab when we're young, and we have to restrain it a lot because serotonin feels good. The urge for social dominance is easy to see in others, but when you feel it yourself, you think you are just trying to survive.

We learn to blame the dominance impulse on "the rich" or on people who act "high and mighty." My professors taught me to blame society, and when I became a professor, I passed this mindset on to my students. But when I learned about the mammal brain, I saw that it was more complicated. Every toddler has the urge to grab and gradually shapes that impulse from its own unique experience. Blaming society for this impulse may please your teachers, but it will not help you understand yourself and your world.

THIS IS NOT HOW I THINK!

You may insist that you do not think this way. Of course, you do not think it in words. You think it with chemicals, and with wiring built from experience.

If you acknowledge your one-up urge, you feel like a bad person, so you focus on the urge in people you don't like. "They are much worse!" you tell yourself. Moral superiority gives you the one-up position, so it feels good. It's hard to get the one-up position in other ways, so moral superiority is highly attractive.

But in the long run, you flood yourself with cortisol when you rely on this finger-pointing mindset. You always feel like a little monkey victimized by bigger monkeys. You think you cannot feel good unless you're a big monkey, and that leads to more cortisol. What's a big-brained mammal to do?

You can recognize the social-comparison thought loops you built in your past, and replace them with healthier thought loops. You can give your inner mammal the one-up position in sustainable ways, and thus enjoy serotonin and relieve cortisol. You can feel good about your strength without being a jerk.

You will keep feeling powerless if you keep blaming the world for your emotions. When you know how you produce your emotions, you can produce something different.

It bears repeating that our goal is not to justify crass competitiveness. Our goal is to explain the gnawing sense of being dominated and transform it into confidence and pride.

You have to recognize your one-up impulse before you can redirect it. We have more words relating to this impulse than Eskimos have for snow. We call it: pride, self-confidence, ego, glory, dominance, power, honor, dignity, self-worth, prestige, prominence, exclusivity, status, social importance, recognition, respect, approval, acclaim, self-aggrandizement, arrogance, assertiveness, manipulativeness, competitiveness, one-upmanship, being special, winning, feeling superior, having class, saving face. We use words with positive connotations for ourselves and those we like, and words with negative connotations for those we don't like.

We need a lot of words for this feeling because our brain goes there a lot. This is not a cosmic flaw. "It's a feature, not a bug" as they say in the tech world. We are alive today because our ancestors did what it took to keep their genes alive in a world of colossal threats. You are not trying to spread your genes, but you have inherited a brain that rewards you with good feelings when you do things that promote reproductive success in the state of nature. That doesn't mean you *should* seek social dominance; it means that you do, and if you hate this impulse, you will end up hating everyone including yourself.

You can learn to manage this impulse instead. By the end of this book, you will manage it better than anyone you know. That's a shameless appeal to your one-up impulse, but you would probably have thought of it anyway!

Quest for Serotonin

Most of what we hear about serotonin is filtered through the disease model. It suggests that serotonin flows effortlessly in "normal" people, and if you lack that effortless flow, you can get it from the health care system. The disease model ignores the natural job of serotonin. Research on serotonin in monkeys suggests that:

- Serotonin evolved to motivate survival action, not to flow all the time for no reason.
- Serotonin produces a calm feeling when an individual sees itself in a position of strength.
- The good feeling prevents conflict by calming those likely to win.
- Neurons connect when serotonin flows, which wires an individual to expect the good feeling in ways that turned it on in their past.
- Serotonin is released in short spurts, so you always have to do more to get more.
- The brain habituates to rewards you have, so a "new and improved" moment of strength is needed to stimulate it.
- When the quest for social dominance is disappointed, cortisol makes it feel like a survival threat.
- Our brain is designed to avoid threats, so it is highly motivated to avoid anything linked to the one-down position in the past.

The disease model creates the illusion that other people are getting serotonin all the time. It seems like "big shots" get it easily, and you are shortchanged. This is false. There is no royal road to serotonin. If you were king of the world, you would not enjoy serotonin every minute. You would worry all the time about losing your status. Kings and emperors always lived in fear of plots against them. Movie stars live in fear of upcoming stars. If you had a spot on the billionaires list, you would fear losing that spot. Cortisol creeps into every life, and it spirals unless you learn to redirect it.

Furthermore, the brain habituates to existing rewards, so any status you have loses its thrill. No matter how high you are, you are still a mammal.

The mammal brain evolved to crave that next serotonin squirt. You think you will be happy forever if you get it, but it is soon metabolized.

Natural selection built a brain designed to keep motivating you. The tabloids hold proof!

Social media is now blamed for these natural impulses. We are invited to blame it whether or not we use it. If you use social media, you are told to blame corporations for making it addictive. If you don't use it, you may feel superior; but when you feel left out, you blame social media for that.

But long before modern technology, humans competed for social importance with whatever technology was available. As soon as a new technology appears, it gets embroiled in the mammalian quest for status. Our ancestors sought "likes" in whatever ways were possible, and probably annoyed their friends and family as they did.

It's hard to get real about your internal process when everyone else blames externals. Opinion leaders court your support by appealing to your one-down feelings and blaming accepted targets. But if you keep blaming externals, you risk having a tabloid life: miserable on the way up and miserable on the way down. You are better off accepting your inner mammal whether or not others get it. Status games are natural. Fear of losing status is natural. But you can be "super-natural" by making peace with your inner mammal.

DIFFERENT GAMES FOR DIFFERENT BRAINS

You may associate status games with fancy watches and fancy titles. You may equate social dominance with people who talk loudly, or get into bar brawls, or visit their money in Switzerland. But status games come in myriad forms because each brain seeks whatever got recognition in its own past. Following are several familiar examples. They will help you see the universal one-up impulse beneath the verbal brain's trappings.

My Car Is Better Than Your Car

Cars, jewelry, artworks, sports equipment, and designer clothing are popular status objects. People want status objects because they feel respected when they display them. This expectation builds because you yourself respect people who have that object. When you acquire the object, you feel good for a while, but soon you notice better objects around you. Now you're one-down, and cortisol tells you to "do something" to relieve it. So you seek the one-up position in the way your brain knows: another status object. Where I live, people with status objects are despised, but that's just another status game, which we might call . . .

My Ethics Are Better Than Your Ethics

Condemning the ethics of others is a convenient way to gain the one-up position. It's free and doesn't waste resources. Best of all, it's low risk because you get to decide who wins. You can always find ethical shortcomings in others and applaud your moral superiority. The serotonin is quickly metabolized, of course, so you need evidence of your superior ethics again and again. "Holier than thou" is the traditional name for this status game. Ironically, moral superiority often goes with self-destructive habits: "I drink because I'm so sensitive to the pain of others." You can justify any addiction by pointing to your concern for the greater good. It's not surprising that so much conversation revolves around the ethical failings of others. We bond with those who share our ethical judgments because it gives our inner mammal the recognition it is looking for. But the more you judge, the more you feel judged. So as ethical as you are, sometimes you long for a more visible manifestation of your superiority, such as . . .

My Abs Are Better Than Your Abs

Animals judge the appearance of others in order to predict their strength. Your mammal brain is always judging the appearance of others, and you presume they are judging you as a result. Each generation finds its own way to keep score. Being fat was a status symbol in the world of food scarcity, and being thin is a status symbol in our world of abundance. Soft hands were a status symbol in the world of manual labor, and now muscles are a status symbol in a world of desk-sitters. Being in better shape than others is a time-honored source of pride. This status game can help us make healthy choices, but it can also lead to harmful extremes, like the tight corsets of earlier generations. When people do stupid things for status, you might prefer the game of . . .

My Intelligence Is Higher Than Your Intelligence

You can rate your own intelligence, but real-world feedback is part of the equation. In the past, intelligence was conveyed by learning Greek and Latin plus another language or two. Today, we define it in many ways, from "street smarts" to coding data-compression algorithms. Test scores and diplomas get attention, but you can find a way to feel smarter than others no matter what your credentials. The good feeling soon passes, alas, so you keep catching others being dumb to keep feeling it. But sometimes you catch yourself being dumb, and your cortisol surges. You feel crushed by smarter people. You urgently look for a form of status that you can control, such as . . .

My Desk Is Neater Than Your Desk

My pie crust is flakier. My batting average is higher. My crops are plowed in straighter rows. These status games are easy to ridicule in others, but taking pride in something you have control over is a useful strategy. Whether it's your well-tended home or your well-tended computer or your well-tended altar to the deities, it's nice to have a reliable source of pride. But the slightest thing out of order triggers one-down feelings when you have this mindset. You urgently look for a way to catch up, and your brain relies on the neural pathways it has. This is why we return to the skills we take pride in, despite the diminishing returns. You may feel like you're on a treadmill, so you long for other ways to feel good. You might notice the ever-popular . . .

My Partner Is Hotter Than Your Partner

It's adolescent, but neuroplasticity peaks in adolescence, so the status games of high school have a big impact on adult emotions. Adults don't like to acknowledge the way they compare partners, but the thought loop is almost irresistible to a brain designed to spread its genes. You evaluate your partner with neural pathways built from your own past experience, so different hotness indicators emerge. When your partner ranks highly, you feel good, as much as you hate to admit it. When they don't measure up, you feel bad, and you may blame them for your bad feeling. You may look for other status games to relieve the tension, such as . . .

I Can Hold My Liquor Better Than You Can

People often take pride in skills that are bad for them. Maybe you can jump from higher cliffs. Maybe you have the best drug dealer. Maybe you pride yourself on how long you can go without sleep. Why would a brain that evolved for survival take pride in skills that are bad for survival? Because social approval promotes survival. If an unhealthy skill won approval in your past, your brain expects a good feeling when you repeat that unhealthy skill. When you try to stop, the loss of social approval feels like a survival threat. It's not surprising that people look for something safe. Perhaps . . .

My Family Is Better Than Your Family

Coming from a "good family" gives you status without lifting a finger. Today, we tend to sneer at this mindset, but if you are honest with yourself, you may notice that your ears perk up when you hear that someone is related to a famous person. Every generation defines status for itself, so the child of a rock star may count as royalty today. Countries with political revolutions typically give status to the children of revolutionaries, thus perpetuating the aristocracy game. It all makes sense when you know that animals compete for partners with good bloodlines. If your family doesn't score on any indicator, you long for a different status game, like . . .

My Hardships Are Harder Than Your Hardships

This status game is ubiquitous today. On the surface it seems strange that a brain designed to seek strength would base status on weakness. But this makes sense from an animal perspective. The size of your social alliances determines your strength in the primate world. Big alliances build when mammals fear a common enemy. In the modern world, thought leaders build big alliances by blaming your hardships on a common enemy. You want to feel oppressed by that enemy so you can be part of the dominant alliance. It's a double bind, alas, since you have to keep feeling bad in order to feel good. You might try to relieve your pain with another status game, such as . . .

My Impact Is Bigger Than Your Impact

Humans are aware of their own mortality, and we terrorize our inner mammal with this knowledge. We relax a bit when we create something that will survive, which is why we long to "have an impact." It takes a lot of self-assertion to have an impact, and that brings the risk of conflict and failure. It's easier if you do it in the name of others. Thus, appeals to the greater good are usually part of the quest to have an impact. The more people you claim to help, the more status you get, which makes this strategy quite appealing. The result is enormous competition to have an impact. If you're exhausted by the competition, you might focus on something tangible, like . . .

My Portfolio Is Bigger Than Your Portfolio

A big asset portfolio can give you a feeling of strength, even if it's private information. You may hate people with assets, and even people who just use the word "portfolio." But stockpiling is a natural survival strategy. Starvation was a real risk for most of human history. In the days before railroads, food was hard to transport so you had to rely on local resources. Our ancestors stockpiled food in order to survive a huge array of potential threats. The bigger their reserves, the safer they felt. It's hard work to accumulate reserves, and you may keep fearing that they're not big enough. So you may be tempted by a time-honored alternative path to one-upness . . .

I Get More Love Than You Get

Everyone compares the love they are getting, as much as we hate to admit it. Children compare the love they get from parents and teachers. Teens compare the love they get at parties. Ancient Roman generals tragically compared the love they got from the public. Punk-music performers compare the love they get to what other punk performers get. You can say you don't compare, but when others get love, your inner mammal notices. Fortunately, you can define love however you want. You can focus on the love of God or the love of your dog. You may have a long string of exes or an entourage of adoring fans. However you define love, your inner mammal wants more. A frail grandma may be getting more from her flock of grandchildren than you are getting from your chosen strategy. But the grandma compares herself to the neighbor who flaunts her own flock of grandchildren, and sometimes feels one-down. It's not surprising that past generations sought status by having more children and even more wives. This mode of social rivalry has obvious drawbacks, so it's nice to have alternatives, such as . . .

My Taste Is Better Than Your Taste

You can sneer at the bad taste of others and applaud the superiority of your own taste. You can put yourself above people with money by pointing out that they spend it with bad taste. You feel good for a moment, and when the serotonin is gone, you can find more *faux pas* in their consumption habits. Recently, the word "creativity" has substituted for "taste." You can feel superior about your creativity whenever you feel one-down. The problem is that you're still keeping score. You're still judging others, so you presume "they" are judging you. Another way to lift yourself up is needed, such as . . .

My Friends Are More Influential Than Your Friends

Name dropping is a well-known path to status. Friends in high places can indeed bring rewards, so they naturally get our attention. A friend of a friend of the big kahuna gets attention regardless of their status on other indicators. Courting people with influence is a long-standing tradition. Monkeys groom the fur of higher-ranking monkeys and it indeed promotes their survival. Early humans gave gifts to high-status individuals because reciprocation is expected. The drive to make contacts and rub elbows with power is easy to see today, though we hate to see it in ourselves. If you can't stand this ritual, you can raise your status by thinking . . .

My Joy Is More Joyous Than Your Joy

People are always telling you what a great time they had, and you wonder if you're missing something. Whether it was their great trip, their great sex, or their great meditation session, your brain compares. Advice-mongers tell us that experience is more valuable than possessions, so our social comparisons come to revolve around fun. However you define it, your brain habituates to what you have, so the same-old thrill loses its effect. It's not surprising that people resort to primal forms of status, like . . .

I Can Control You

Waiting in line at the Department of Motor Vehicles can trigger one-down feelings. No matter how much power you have in the rest of your life, you may feel powerless in that moment. People seek one-up positions in whatever ways are available to them. However, you may have landed in the DMV line because you did something dumb; and that's painful to think about, so you blame your one-down feeling on "them." We are not objective judges of our social environment. It's easy to presume that your waiter is snubbing you when you are feeling one-down anyway. We suspect others of one-upping us because we know the urge so well. Fortunately, you have the self-restraint to avoid escalating to . . .

I Can Inflict More Pain Than You Can

The impulse to win at any price is not socially acceptable. We learn to control that impulse to sustain social bonds. If you grab a toy from an-other child, you are taught to restrain that impulse. If you bite the child who grabbed your toy, you learn from feedback. Self-restraint must be learned because our brain is inherited from a world in which inflicting pain was the coin of the realm. Thus, we fear the strength of others and long for the strength to protect ourselves. Social norms evolve to manage this impulse, such as: "My lawyer is better than your lawyer." If you don't have the strength to win in this way, there's always the inverse strategy. . .

I Can Tolerate More Pain Than You Can

I need less sleep. I need less food. I need less money. You know this game. I deny myself, and you must deny yourself more or else I win. Of course, it doesn't feel great even when you win, so it's nice to win with a more cerebral strategy like . . .

My Predictions Are Better Than Your Predictions

Predicting may not seem like a path to status, but we do it all the time. Whether you predict the stock market, the big game, the election, or the weather, you feel proud when you're right. Predicting is the unique capacity of the human cortex, so we have a deep sense of its importance. Our ancestors survived by predicting the behavior of predators and prey. They strived to predict rain with a great sense of urgency. Today, we strive to predict which start-up will take off, which post will go viral, which athlete or politician will score, and what will happen to life on earth. Gambling, video games, the lottery, chess, and technology forecasting are other popular ways to feel superior about your predicting skills. Dopamine is also stimulated by correct predictions, and the double dose of happy chemicals gives us double motivation for prediction games. If your prediction proves wrong, you can fall back on the most basic of status games . . .

They're All Jerks

Blanket condemnations are a fast, easy way to claim the one-up position. You focus on the flaws of others and pride yourself on your perceptiveness. You enjoy a one-up moment each time you find flaws in those you perceive as stronger than yourself. And when the good feeling passes, you berate them again. This thought loop is widespread, so it's easily learned from others. You are welcomed into the club if you hate the same "jerks" that they hate. Mammals bond when predators lurk, and the mammal brain rewards you with oxytocin when you find social support. Serotonin is added when your alliance is stronger than their alliance. The double reward makes it enormously tempting to bond around common enemies, whether in politics, sports, career, or a daily gripe session. Saying "they're all jerks" is a fast, easy way to meet your social needs.

YOU HAVE A CHOICE

Status games feel like the fault of others because it's easier to see the one-up urges of others than to see your own. This makes it easy to conclude that others are putting you down, so you don't have a choice.

Your brain zooms in on small perceived advantages in others, and cortisol makes it feel like an emergency. Repetition builds a cortisol pathway that helps you slide into this thought loop. Fortunately, we have billions of extra neurons to build new thought loops. The following chapters show you how.

LEARNING FROM HISTORY

Most chapters of this book end with the status games of a famous person in history. I chose these people because I visited their homes and felt their status frustrations while standing in their living rooms. These homes are open to the public, so you can do it too!

The point of these stories is not that fame is good. Nor is it that fame is bad. The point is that everyone has ups and downs because serotonin is soon gone, and we want more. This is the engine of human history.

The status frustrations of other times and places help us see past the status frustrations of our own time and place. When you see the same patterns everywhere, it's easier to see the mammalian universals underneath. This makes it easier to accept yourself and others. You can enjoy the world you live in instead of cursing it and spiraling with cortisol. People have always felt dominated by others and looked for ways to come out ahead. We can learn from the ways others manage this universal frustration.

THE STATUS GAMES OF CHARLES DARWIN

I was thrilled when I learned that Darwin's home is open to the public. I rushed to the London suburb and stared at the desk where he wrote. I walked the path where he took his daily stroll and explored the greenhouse where he fertilized his orchids. All the while, I wondered how he managed the status games in his life.

I knew the familiar story about Darwin: that he was oppressed by religion and triumphed with a merry band of influential pals. It made me think, "where is my merry band of influential pals?" But I kept researching and found that his story was more complex.

Science and religion were not seen as opponents in Darwin's time. On the contrary, Darwin trained for the ministry in order to pursue his interest in "natural philosophy." Darwin's opponents were people whose status was threatened by his work. Darwin was meek and had no stomach for public battles, so his final triumph is quite heartening.

The story begins with the amazing fact that Darwin's grandfather thought of evolution. Erasmus Darwin was a doctor and a friend of Benjamin Franklin. He suggested evolution in the long poem he wrote about reproduction in nature. The poem was considered scandalous. It was popular, but the science world ignored it. Erasmus died before Charles was born, but Charles was expected to become a doctor like his father and grandfather. He was sent to medical school at age fifteen. After watching surgery on a child before the invention of anesthesia, he refused to go to class. He spent his time in the way he always had: by observing nature.

While he was out watching birds, insects, and sea creatures, he met others doing the same. He met a professor, and his knowledge and enthusiasm impressed the distinguished naturalist. That led to his post as naturalist on the *Beagle*.

You may think he had an easy life, but his hardships were severe. When he was nine, his mother died, and his father packed him off to boarding school. His father ridiculed his nature-watching and vetoed the offer to sail around the world on the *Beagle*. When young Charles finally got his father's permission, he faced the true hardship of such a voyage. Darwin was seasick most of the time, and ill for the rest of his life with afflictions believed to have come from the voyage.

Darwin's status conflict with the captain of the *Beagle* is a fascinating story. Captain Fitzroy sought a young-gentleman naturalist to share his cabin because protocol prevented captains from socializing with the crew. Fitzroy got lonely and depressed on long voyages, and Charles was destined to be his audience.

But things turned sour because Charles's sisters sent his letters home to London newspapers, which made him an instant celebrity. The news reached the *Beagle* while it was still on the other side of the world! Captain Fitzroy was jealous. He had no home of his own because he was orphaned in youth and had lived on a ship since age fourteen. So instead of returning to London in two years as planned, he stretched the voyage into five years. Imagine Charles tossed on the high seas in a tiny cabin with this man for five years. To make matters worse, Fitzroy forbade Charles from publishing a trip journal except as a chapter of Fitzroy's journal.

When they finally returned to London, Charles was the toast of society. Everyone wanted to hear about his trip. But Darwin was shy and preferred to live in the country and study the animal artifacts he'd brought home. So he did that for twenty years. He kept thinking about evolution, but never felt that his explanation was ready for public scrutiny.

Then, he was ensnared by one of history's great coincidences. The mailman brought an envelope with an essay from a young man, requesting that Darwin get it published. The essay said precisely what Darwin had been thinking all these years.

What should he do?

If he had tossed the letter into the fireplace, no one would have known, because the young man had no ties to the science establishment.

If he had it published, Alfred Russell Wallace would get credit for the concept of evolution by natural selection, since Darwin had never gone on record.

Wallace was a man who made his living by collecting wildlife specimens from rainforests worldwide and selling them to researchers and collectors. He had a life of extreme hardship but managed to spend a lot of time observing animals in their natural habitat. He drew his own insights and dared to write them down. His historic essay was actually written while he was suffering a malarial delirium in Borneo.

Darwin did the honorable thing—he reported the essay to his friends in the science community. They came up with a plan: a public science meeting where an essay from each man would be presented. Darwin wrote something fast, but on the day of the meeting, he was sadly attending his child's funeral. Wallace was still in Asia trying to make a living. Both essays were unceremoniously read into the record.

At this point, my belief was that Darwin won acceptance because his friends rallied around him. This is what our inner mammal dreams of. But the truth was more complicated. Some of Darwin's alleged friends did not support him, and his biggest supporters were people who were advancing their own agenda and not really friends. Darwin was a mammal among mammals like the rest of us. He hated politics, but he kept working.

Three of Darwin's children died during this work. He blamed himself for this because he had married his first cousin. Such marriages were common before the discovery of DNA, and Queen Victoria had married her first cousin around the time that the Darwins did. But Charles understood genetics because he socialized with animal breeders. He saw the consequences of inbreeding in domestic animals even though he didn't know the mechanism of genetics. He suffered from constant stomach pain and feared that his frailty was inherited by his children.

Darwin kept working despite this hardship and despite his wife's vehement opposition. She cried over his "blasphemy." It would keep him out of heaven she feared, and thus separate them for eternity.

Part 1

WHY STATUS GAMES
ARE RELENTLESS

Chapter One

Status Games in Animals

When two mammals meet, one makes a dominance gesture and the other makes a submission gesture. A dominance gesture might be an erect posture with a direct stare. Once one individual asserts dominance, the other must submit or risk a fight. Animals rarely fight because they are good at predicting who would win. The weaker individual submits to avoid injury, typically by lowering its head or body. With that uncomfortable business out of the way, two mammals can avoid conflict and even cooperate.

Animals defer to the more dominant individual when food or mating opportunity appears. Fights over resources are rare because the pecking order has already been established. You may think it shouldn't be this way, but a century of research shows that it is. Countless studies in "ethology" have documented the hierarchical behavior of animals. Today, this research is ignored, and studies purporting to show altruism and empathy in animals are spotlighted. Such studies carve out moments of cooperation and omit the larger context, which shows that animals compete when it helps raise their status.

For example, animals cooperate to take down a more dominant rival. If they succeed, they compete for the rival's position. Cooperation is part of the status game. Animals are skilled at judging the strength of a social alliance in the same way that they can judge the strength of an individual. Humans have used social alliances in this way throughout history, and we still do today. The point here is not to justify aggression but to know why we are hypersensitive to perceived differences in strength.

Mammals have social rivalry because it works. It enables weaker individuals to enjoy the protection of stronger individuals in the face of common enemies. Each brain strives to rise in the hierarchy by building strength and skill. It helps them get more food and mating opportunity, and thus spread their genes. This applies to females as well as males, as we'll see. A brain that seeks status is more likely to be inherited. We are all descendants of millions of years of status seeking.

We often hear about the "alpha" of an animal group. That word is not used in this book except when it appears in an original source, because it suggests that status seeking is a characteristic of some individuals and not others. The fact is that every brain strives to advance itself. There are always plenty of "betas" vying for the top spot when the incumbent weakens or dies. And plenty of "middling sorts" vying for the beta spots. Instead of blaming status seeking on a certain personality type, it's important to see that each individual is motivated to assert itself as soon as it sees that it could win. Different species have different social-rivalry rituals, but the common pattern is overwhelming.

WHY ANIMALS SEEK STATUS

Animals are constantly deciding whether to assert themselves or hold back. They make these decisions with a very small cortex. An ape's prefrontal cortex is about a third the size of a human's, a monkey's is about a tenth, and other animals have much less. Animals make social decisions without listing pros and cons or wishing things were different. They respond to social situations with neurochemicals wired by past experience. Let's see how this works for a young monkey.

Every monkey starts life in a position of extreme weakness. It survives thanks to an oxytocin bond with its mother. But she won't live forever, and she must invest in other offspring to keep her genes alive. A mother monkey never feeds her child except for milk, so the little monkey must learn to feed itself. Its mirror neurons initiate the action of reaching for food when it sees others doing that. Once it tastes the food, dopamine surges and it feels good. Dopamine is the brain's signal that a need has been met. Neurons connect when dopamine flows, which wires a young monkey to repeat behaviors that meet its needs.

At first, the little monkey just grabs without social awareness. Nature protects it with juvenile markings like a tuft of white head fur. A little monkey can push and grab with impunity as long as it has juvenile markings. Once those markings fade, it is treated like anyone else. Stronger monkeys will grab food from its hands, and even its mouth. If it resists, it is bitten, and that wires it to restrain itself near stronger individuals. Pain is a big surge of cortisol. Neurons connect when cortisol flows, which builds a neural pathway that turns on the bad feeling the next time the little monkey thinks of grabbing food in the presence of a bigger monkey.

Hunger motivates a young monkey to find food that is not dominated by a bigger monkey. Dopamine circuits help it scan for opportunity. If it sees something in the distance, dopamine motivates an approach. But as a little monkey distances itself from others, its oxytocin falls. It loses that nice feeling of protection, and its cortisol alarm blares. Now it has a tough choice. The little brain weighs the threat of hunger against the threat of predation. It does this without words or complex cognition—it uses neural pathways built from past neurochemical experience. Some little monkeys get eaten, but enough of them survive to keep the species alive.

A little monkey is not at the bottom of the hierarchy forever. One fine day, it sees a fruit near a troop mate that is smaller. Serotonin is released, and the good feeling eases its fear of asserting itself. It has no ill will toward the smaller monkey. It just wants to relieve its hunger without big risks. It understands its own strength because it wrestles a lot. When it prevails in a tussle, a nice shot of serotonin is released. Neurons connect when serotonin flows, and its brain learns to expect more good feelings in similar future contexts.

No abstract concept of status is needed for a young brain to wire in status consciousness. The brain's electricity flows easily along neurons that were activated before, but it has trouble flowing down neurons that have not been developed by past activation. Thus, relying on past experience is literally the path of least resistance. Without conscious intent, the mammal brain constantly compares its strength to others and anticipates pleasure or pain by releasing the appropriate chemical.

Social rivalry intensifies when a little monkey reaches puberty. Sex hormones expand its reward-seeking behavior. New pathways build as new assertions succeed or fail. Here again, no conscious intent is needed. Brains that rewarded self-assertion with a good feeling made more copies of themselves. Brains that responded to social setbacks with a survival-threat feeling survived. This is the brain we've inherited. You may find it hard to believe because it's not what you hear elsewhere and because it conflicts with more comforting notions of peace and love in the state of nature. You may be wondering what to believe.

WHY HAVEN'T I HEARD THIS?

We hear a lot of research on empathy and altruism in animals. I learned in school that the state of nature is peaceful and "our society" causes dominance-seeking. I taught that myself as a college professor. I had learned to equate that belief with virtue and intelligence, so I feared seeming stupid and evil if I questioned it. But the more I learned, the more I questioned social science orthodoxies about the state of nature.

For most of human history, people would not believe you if you said that animals are altruistic because they could see wild animals for themselves. Today, it's hard to see wild animals in action so we are easily persuaded by a few studies that get widely reported. Information that conflicts with these studies is not widely available. But over the years, bits of conflicting information kept snagging my attention until I could not ignore it. Here are some examples:

- A wildcat sanctuary near my home was soliciting contributions. They asked me to support their sanctuary to save wildcats that wander into the suburbs. I asked why wildcats were put in a sanctuary instead of being returned to the wild. I had to ask a few times to get an answer. Finally, they said that a rereleased wildcat would be killed by the wildcat whose territory it was released into. The good people who promote the sanctuary are reluctant to reveal the inconvenient truth behind the need for it.
- A prominent veterinarian advises cat owners to buy separate food and toys for each cat and place them where no other cat can see. The good doctor is too nice to give the reason: Stronger cats try to dominate

the resources of weaker cats, even when they have plenty of food and toys of their own.

- Jane Goodall introduced the world to a young chimpanzee she named Flint. It is widely reported that Flint died of a broken heart after his mother died. This is often represented as evidence of love and empathy in the state of nature. The truth is much harsher. Flint died because he never learned to meet is own survival needs. Flint did not grow up in the natural state because he was the first chimp to grow up with Jane's "provisioning" of bananas. He failed to wire in the food-seeking skills that normal chimps take five years to build. Jane is not to blame, since she could not have known what we know today thanks to her efforts. What matters is Flint's response to his brave new world. When he reached normal weaning age, he was stronger than his mother because she was elderly and he was fortified by bananas. When his mother "Flo" tried to withhold her milk, he overpowered her. Bullying his own mother allowed him to keep nursing throughout his years of neuroplasticity. These facts are in the public record, but they are ignored because they conflict with cherished visions of animals. Jane stopped provisioning chimps as soon as she understood the consequences, but most people still cling to the romantic view of nature. They pride themselves on their intelligence as they choose one slice of information and ignore the rest.

DOMINANCE HIERARCHY IN ANIMALS

Today, teachers and media represent animals as compassionate beings, but the conflict among animals was well known to twentieth-century researchers. The evidence is still available to anyone who looks for it.

The term "pecking order" was coined a century ago by a Norwegian zoologist who grew up with chickens. Thorleif Schjelderup-Ebbe noticed that one chicken always ate first and drove others away from the best pieces of food. He saw how chickens held back until stronger individuals ate, always ending up in the same order. When two strange chickens were put together, huge squabbles erupted, and then one individual gradually put up less resistance until they appeared to coexist peacefully. When a flock had more than thirty chickens, they were unable to remember the pecking order, and endless conflict erupted.

Schjelderup-Ebbe's 1921 PhD dissertation was a methodical study of behaviors he'd observed since age ten.

Nobel Laureate Konrad Lorenz expanded this work to other animals, and learned that most squabbling occurs between individuals of similar rank. Researchers went on to find the same dominance behaviors in dozens of species. They noticed that primates challenge the hierarchy more often than smaller-brained mammals. Herd animals tend to fight each other once and stick with the outcome as long as their leader endures. If their leader dies or is overthrown, everyone fights everyone else until a new order is established. Primates, by contrast, will challenge the hierarchy whenever they think they can win. They have enough neurons to update their mental model based on the outcome. A primate's brain will even record changes in the relative status of two other individuals in the group.

It's hard for us to see dominance hierarchies the way animals do because our big cortex creates abstractions. Monkeys do not think abstractly about "making it to the top." They just strive to trigger good feelings and avoid bad feelings. A window into their mindset has come to us by a fascinating laboratory accident. Researchers returned a monkey to its troop after a medical procedure without realizing that the anesthesia hadn't fully worn off. The young monkey was less quick witted than usual, and its troop mates immediately pounced on the subtle signs of weakness. A bully bit it repeatedly, and other monkeys joined in, including its regular playmate. The researchers realized what was happening and quickly took the hapless critter out. They were stunned at the ugliness that a momentary weakness could provoke. Two hours later, the monkey recovered fully from the anesthesia and was returned to the troop. This time it responded to provocations with appropriate signals, and normal social interactions resumed (Maestripieri, *Macachiavellian Intelligence*, 125–26).

Stories like this may upset you because they trigger your early experience with social dominance. Your anger may surge at the thought of a bully, and you eagerly root for the underdog. But when underdogs prevail, they act the same way that their predecessors did. So instead of yielding to simplistic notions of good guys and bad guys, it's useful to remember the contributions that go with social dominance. Dominant mammals provide protection from predators, resolve conflicts in the group, and share resources. Their ability to do this is enhanced by the extra food and deference they get. When you stereotype dominants and nondominants, you miss their common core. Each brain is just doing what it can to spread its genes because that feels good. When you understand this common core, your emotions make sense, and so do the emotions of others. You can navigate toward more good feelings and avoid more bad feelings.

The idea that dominants "share" requires some clarification. When a dominant chimp asserts control over a resource, they may not actually want it. If they have all the food and mating opportunities they need at the moment, they offer the surplus to their allies. This strengthens their alliances and thus helps sustain their dominance. Everyone notices the rewards that come from supporting the dominant individual. The expectation of reward motivates a rush to support the dominant. To call this "sharing" is to cover up the harsh facts of life with a Rousseauian veneer.

You may find it hard to imagine animals competing for food because we're trained to think their food is free for the taking. It helps to explore the competition for reproductive opportunity, which means everything relevant to the survival of your genes, from high-quality mates to rich milk to protection from predators.

NO FREE LOVE IN THE STATE OF NATURE

You may think love is easily available to animals, but they actually work hard for any "reproductive success" that comes their way. Males work hard for the muscles necessary to succeed in the mating game, and females work to produce strong children and keep them alive. Food-seeking skills are central to producing muscles and rich milk, but social skills are central as well. The stakes are high. A male could get shut out of mating opportunities, and a female could watch her child get eaten alive.

Animals who raise their status make more copies of their genes. No knowledge of genetics is necessary for a status-seeking brain to spread. Mammals just do what feels good, and status games result. Here are some fascinating mating games that show how this works.

A farmer introduced me to the animal facts of life. He gave me a tour of his prized herd of organic cows, and mentioned the bulls that he rents at breeding time. I asked him why he rents bulls since his cows surely give birth to males. He said that intact males are too aggressive to manage on a farm, so specialists are needed to handle them. When rented bulls are released into his barnyard, the most dominant bull heads straight to the center of the herd, while the other bulls array themselves around the edges. Paternity tests show that 70 percent of the young have the same dad.

At the time, I was studying to be a docent at my local zoo. I had just been taught that female bovines push their way to the center of the herd for safety from predators. As a cow weakens with age, she ends up around the edges where she's exposed to predators. She may have had center stage when she was young, and thus kept her offspring in relative safety. After a lifetime of pushing, her genes will live on, and the next generation will keep pushing.

As I stood with the farmer watching his cows, I connected the dots: At the center of the herd, the pushiest boy meets the pushiest girl. I shared this insight with my Hollywood niece at a family gathering, and she connected dots of her own. She suddenly understood why her peers wait in lines outside trendy nightclubs: "They expect to meet a 'ten' inside!" The point is not that we should hang around nightclubs or push others out of our way. The point is that our brains urgently seek everything we associate with "reproductive success," even when we're not trying to reproduce.

My animal mating education continued in France's Monkey Valley (La Vallée des Singes). At this all-primate zoo, keepers give lectures on social behavior. At the baboon exhibit, I heard a keeper say that lower-ranking males do not reproduce. I was surprised, and wondered if I had misunderstood the French. So after the talk, I asked if it was really true that lower-ranking males never have sex. The keeper replied that they have sex, but they do not become fathers. What?!? My French was not good enough to clarify this enigma, so I decided to research it when I got home. I learned that male mammals are not especially interested in females unless the smell of ovulation is in the air (with the exception of humans and bonobos). But in the first days of estrus, a female baboon is not yet fertile. A mature male of experience can tell by the pheromones when it's worth risking conflict. Before that, he doesn't interfere when lower-ranking males take initiative. Thus, a male may gain experience, but he will not actually keep his genes alive unless he raises his status.

I was amazed that La Vallée des Singes was offering the real facts of life in public, so I went back as soon as I could. The next time, I learned a huge lesson at the mandrill exhibit. Mandrills have beautiful rainbow stripes on the snouts and bottoms of males. They look like baboons otherwise, so I asked the keeper if their behavior is similar. She said they are less violent than baboons because they compete with color instead of aggression. She pointed to a picture of wild mandrills and explained that their colors are brighter in the wild because there's more competition. Wild mandrills live in large troops where many males compete, and bright colors are needed to attract the ladies. In the zoo troop, males were few, thus little competition and little color.

This seemed like the Rosetta Stone of life! Competing over appearances is not bad when you think of it as a substitute for violence. Baboon violence is nasty due to their huge canine teeth. Mandrills evolved a beautiful alternative. When I learned the whole story, however, it seemed less benign. Male displays come at a price. Research shows that when females select for a trait, it is indeed a valid indicator of "fitness." From a moose's antlers to a peacock's tail to an orangutan's cheek pads, the desired trait always correlates with social dominance.

Animals are amazingly picky about their mating partners because the survival of their young depends on it. They invest great effort in everything that affects their access to high-ranking partners. You may think this is just male behavior and would not happen in a world run by females. So let's explore the intense status games of matriarchal mammals.

WOMEN ON TOP

Female status comes in many varieties. In some mammals, females dominate the group; while in others, females have their own status hierarchy within a male-dominated group. Another common pattern is an all-female hierarchy with males living alone. Yet other species live in groups ruled by a power couple, and others live in couples with no group at all. These diverse lifestyles have a common core: Females cooperate when it promotes their genes, and they're aggressive when that promotes their genes—just like males.

For example, meerkats are led by a female who fights her way to the top. Once in charge, she selects her male consort, and together they prevent the rest of the gang (that's the correct collective noun) from reproducing. The queen attacks any female who goes near a male, and her consort attacks any male who goes near a female. The queen will kill any child other than hers who manages to get born. The whole gang thus revolves around the offspring of the top girl. This is called "cooperative" child-rearing by people who shape the facts to fit their lens and omit the rest of the story.

Hyenas are a female-dominated species with a unique form of aggression. They birth twins most of the time, and the first one born kills the second if both are female. To get the full picture, it's essential to know that female hyenas have the external appearance of males. Their clitoris is enlarged and they have two fatty spheres, thus creating the appearance of a male without the functionality. It seems like natural selection favored females with an appearance that helps them survive a predatory older sister, without sacrificing the aggression hyenas need to compete with lions and cheetahs.

Elephants live in all-female groups. Boys leave home at puberty due to some combination of expulsion and wanderlust. But the result in not what you associate with "girl power." Female elephants line up in age order and spend their lives following their older relatives with every step. (A curious exception is the reverse ordering of daughters, putting the youngest next to the mother and giving the oldest a chance to learn parenting skills.) If you were a female elephant, you would never make a decision until everyone in front of you died. This has survival value because the oldest individual has the longest memory of where to find water in a drought. A herd of elephants is often idealized as "working together for the common good." This ignores the complete submission at the heart of their lifestyle.

Macaque monkeys live in large groups with female-dominated status hierarchies. Researchers found that girls tend to end up at about the same status level as their mothers. This was called "inheriting" status, but a closer look showed the learned behavior involved. Every young female starts out at the bottom of the hierarchy, but if her mother is high in rank, she learns high-ranking behaviors. She takes initiatives and tolerates risk more than other girls because she expects it to work. She makes more dominance gestures and fewer submission gestures. Her mother sides with her. She ends up with more conflict but also more food, which builds more strength.

Female chimpanzees have their own hierarchy within male-dominated troops. They follow the highest-ranking female when they go out to forage. When the leading lady finds a fruit tree, she takes the best spot in front of it and the other ladies gather around in rank order. The low-ranking ladies end up with less food and more exposure to predators. If a low-ranking lady is too pushy, she is bitten by the huge canine teeth of a stronger lady. But if she is not pushy enough, she's malnourished, which leads to weaker mating partners and weaker babies. She cannot forage alone, due to the high risk of attack by neighboring chimp troops. So she constantly scans for opportunities to ingratiate herself with the mean girls, and her brain is designed to do that!

You may be wondering about bonobos, the allegedly kinder and gentler ape. Bonobo troops are female dominated in an interesting way. Females are only about 10 percent smaller than males, whereas female chimps are about a third smaller. Any two female bonobos can win a conflict with a male if they stick together—and they do. But they have not built a utopia with this power. They have built a hierarchical system that's eerily similar to the Spartan army. In ancient Sparta, a young soldier had to serve a higher-ranking soldier to gain status. Sexual gratification was one of his duties. Female bonobos have the same kind of "mentorship." They transfer in from other troops at puberty and attach themselves to a high-ranking female to whom they submit totally.

You may have heard that bonobos and chimpanzees have "orgies." That conclusion is easy to reach from the far end of binoculars, but systematic study reveals that the festivities are actually status games.

THE TRUTH ABOUT PROMISCUITY

Biologists call bonobos and chimpanzees "promiscuous." That word had no sexual or moral connotation when the label first appeared. In Latin, it means "crowded." If you say, "This is a promiscuous beach" in French, it means "this is a crowded beach." The term "promiscuous species" was a polite euphemism when biologists used it to distinguish chimp mating patterns from those of "monogamous species," "harem species," and "tournament species." Let's peak inside the promiscuous world to see what really goes on.

Male chimpanzees are only interested in sex when a female is actively fertile, and that only happens once in five years because a newborn is nursed for four years. When the big moment finally comes, the strongest male engages in what biologists call "mate guarding." He follows her around and blocks access for other guys' genetic material. He makes exceptions for his allies, however—the strong males who fight alongside him when the group is attacked. To be part of the in-crowd, a male must court the male power structure for years. Or he can risk his life on a quickie when the power players are busy elsewhere. Biologists call this "sneaky copulation."

The female is motivated to mate with as many males as possible because that brings more protection for herself and her child in the future. But the male honcho will bite her if she chooses someone who's not on his list. She is always alert for opportunities to promote her interests without getting bitten.

The word "partying" is often used to describe a chimp troop in estrus, but this is serious business to the participants. A male chimp spends years climbing the ladder in order to be in a position of power when opportunity knocks. The climb was all for nothing if he is booted out before his genes are immortalized. Some chimps commit infanticide because that speeds things along by ending lactation. They will never kill the child of a female they've had contact with, however, which explains the females' commitment to diversity. When females solicit partners to prevent infanticide, I would not call it "partying" or "free love." It is currying favor with high-status individuals to advance one's children—a behavior well-known to humans.

Occasionally, two females are in estrus at the same time. The competition that results is not what you'd expect, because male chimps are curiously partial to older females. Research shows higher survival rates in the children of more experienced mothers. Younger females end up in the undignified position of clamoring for the attention of the top-ranking males. What looks like a party to casual observers is actually a collection of individuals promoting themselves. We've all been to that kind of party!

Bonobos are known as the "hippie chimp" because they "make love, not war." To be blunt, they are known for genital rubbing in every imaginable configuration. Research shows that bonobos rub genitals to prevent conflict and to restore peace after conflict erupts. If you get in the way of a stronger bonobo, you can protect yourself from aggression by rubbing the stronger one's genitals. I would not call this "love." It's the opposite of love.

Bonobos are surprisingly competitive over mating opportunity, considering its easy availability. The competition takes an unusual form: Females compete to be with the sons of high-ranking females. This is akin to human empresses who gave their sons many mistresses or concubines. It's hard to get the full facts about bonobos because they are few in number and live in high-conflict regions. But the facts we have are amazingly consistent with the mammalian pattern of seeking status to promotes one's genes.

POWER COUPLES AND THE SEXY SON HYPOTHESIS

Different status games emerge from different ecological niches. It's fascinating to see how each game is adaptive for specific environments. Monogamy is adaptive under some conditions, and tournaments work in others. Each behavior is the sweet spot in the quest to get rewards and avoid harm in that niche.

Monogamy is the norm for gibbons. Once they form pair bonds, they stake out a territory large enough to feed their children. They defend that territory from other gibbons in interesting ways. Each morning when they wake up, they sing a duet for half an hour, with specific male and female parts. Their hoots warn other gibbons to stay away, like the bumper sticker that says, "If you can read this, you're too close." Their sound projects through the rain forest thanks to a throat sac that expands to the size of their head. If they sound weak, other gibbons are tempted to intrude. If a male gibbon intrudes, the male of the couple tries to kill it, and if a female intrudes, the female attacks it. To us, rain forests look lush, but gibbons see their children starve if their territory is too small or too crowded. If their territory is too large, they can't defend it and deadly conflict results. Singing spaces them out in a way that's just right.

Wolf packs have power couples. Each pack is led by a dominant male and female who sustain their dominance with methods that should not surprise you by now. The dominant female bites her female pack mates if they go near a male, though they are typically her relatives and even her children. This aggression stresses the subordinate females to the point that they stop cycling. The dominant male exercises the same dominion over his male pack mates. In this way, the whole pack works to support the children of the lead pair. Again, this is glamorized as "cooperative child-rearing," which misrepresents the underlying impulses. You may wonder why the nondominant wolves stick around. They do leave when food is abundant, but in their sparse environment, starvation is common among those who leave. A few "lone wolves" survive, and they go on to start their own packs and preserve their own genes. Many stick with the safety of the group, waiting for an opportunity that may never come.

Tournament species use open combat as their mate-choice mechanism. Males go head-to-head while a female stands by to see who wins. Males have thick skulls in tournament species because they charge at their rivals with full force. You may have heard that big antlers are "just for show," but if you watch video of these contests, the ferocity is clear. Watch male kangaroos, deer, sea lions, or elephants, and you will wonder how they survive to compete again in the next rutting season.

The tournament system depends on the female's willingness to go with the winner. What does she see in the brute? Survival rates for babies are low in the state of nature, and there's little a mother can do to raise the odds except to choose the best paternal genes.

Combat drains a species' energy, so nonviolent alternatives have evolved. In some species, females just choose the male they see other females with. Biologists call this "mate choice copying." They explain it with the "sexy son hypothesis." The reproductive potential of females is quite limited compared to males, but a female can even the score if her sons are attractive to other females. The best way to have a sexy son is to choose an attractive father. This theory upsets people who want animals to fit their belief system. But in daily life, it's easy to see young women concentrating their attentions on a limited subset of males. It's nice to think of this behavior as an improvement over violent competition.

Elephants have evolved an amazing way to minimize their brutal tournaments. Male elephants actually have hormone cycles. Once or twice a year, a male's testosterone rises to colossal levels, and he becomes so aggressive that other males yield to him no matter what his size. The result is genetic diversity for the next generation and fewer skull-crunching dominance contests.

IT STARTS YOUNG

Animals build status-seeking skills long before puberty. Pigs are an extreme example. A mother pig with eight teats can birth twelve infants, so her piglets must compete or starve from the moment of birth. They latch onto a teat and defend it from others. When they're strong enough, they strive for a better teat—one closer to the mother's heart, where it's warmer and the fat content is higher. Piglets of both sexes kill their siblings when they have the strength to do so. An hour after birth, the competition stops, and each piglet retains its position for good. A poem explaining these facts was written by two researchers:

> A piglet's most precious possession
> Is the teat that he fattens his flesh on.
> He fights for his teat with tenacity
> Against any sibling's audacity.
> The piglet, to arm for this mission,
> Is born with a warlike dentition
> Of eight tiny tusks, sharp as sabres,
> Which help in impressing the neighbors;
> But to render these weapons less harrowing,
> Most farmers remove them at farrowing.
> We studied pig sisters and brothers
> When some had their teeth, but not others.
> We found that when siblings aren't many,
> The weapons help little if any,
> But when there are many per litter,
> The teeth help their owners grow fitter.
> But how did selection begin
> To make weapons to use against kin?
> (Abstract from the paper "Armed Sibling Rivalry
> among Suckling Piglets" by Fraser and Thompson)

The mammal brain cares about status as if its life depends on it because in the state of nature, it does. In the animal world, status is akin to saving money for a rainy day. On a good day, an animal may have extra energy left after it meets its survival needs. How can it invest today's surplus in a way that helps it survive tomorrow? By raising its status. It could do that by grooming a potential ally, or protecting the child of a potential ally, or even by challenging a rival instead of submitting.

Before money was invented, status was the primary path to security. Investing effort in a way that accumulates the respect of peers leads to more nutrition and more reproductive success. Status games are less frustrating when you understand the drives that fuel them.

THE CENTER OF ATTENTION

Field research shows that animals focus their attention on the high-status individuals in their group. Laboratory research shows that monkeys will actually "pay" for the privilege of looking at pictures of their group leaders. Researchers gave monkeys the opportunity to exchange food tokens for a peek at some photos. When the photos depicted fertile females, headlines were made, and the study was depicted as the origin of pornography. But the monkeys also paid to look at prestige members of their group, which seems like the origin of tabloids.

Horses help us understand the link between status and attention. When you see a group of horses, the leader is not the one in the front, but the one in the center. This happens because horses try to follow the strongest individual, and that individual has pushed its way to the center for its own benefit. The dominant leads from the center because the others keep watching it.

When you are with a group, you may feel like certain people are the center of attention. It's not surprising that humans compete for attention and feel so one-down when they're overlooked. People strive to relieve that bad feeling by raising their social standing. These impulses are nonverbal, but our verbal brain can understand them by exploring the status games of early humans.

THE STATUS GAMES OF JANE AUSTEN

Jane Austen's novels made it respectable to marry for love instead of status. When I heard that Jane's home was open to the public, I couldn't wait to step into her world. I was shocked by what I learned, however. The tour guide said that Jane never found love herself. I wanted to know more, so I visited some of the many "Jane slept here" spots in southern England, and then did a lot of research.

Modern Austen biographies promote the feminist idea that Jane didn't care about marriage. But since her books are all about marriage, it's fair to say that the subject was on her mind. Let's consider an alternative explanation for her celibacy: Jane had a bad case of status anxiety. While her verbal brain talked about love, her nonverbal brain was so status obsessed that, like Groucho Marx, she could never accept an affiliation with someone who would stoop to accept her.

Jane's parents also had a bad case of status anxiety. They lived in a culture where wealthy families preserved their estates by bequeathing everything to the eldest son. That left other siblings stranded. Jane's parents had been stranded thus. They had no way to support themselves in the style to which they had become accustomed. Working for money was considered demeaning, and you feared being shunned by "society" if you did. Military or church careers were acceptable, but the pay was low. Thus, many "society" people could barely survive. Jane's family was among them.

Jane's father was a clergyman. He had a coveted spot as the rector of lands owned by his cousin. The rectory had a guaranteed income because contributions to the church were required by law. But it was not much money for a family with seven children like the Austens, especially with a socially ambitious mum like Jane's.

Jane grew up feeling poor because her mother felt poor, and because she always had rich cousins to compare herself to. Jane's mother also grew up comparing herself to rich people. Jane's grandfather was a rector at Oxford, and his salary was far below the family income of students at Oxford. Jane's mother spent a lot of time courting rich relatives in hopes of finding opportunities for her children. She succeeded spectacularly in some ways. Two of her sons became heirs to huge estates thanks to relatives with no sons of their own. Jane spent a lot of time on these estates, further solidifying her aristocratic expectations.

What are a girl's options in that world? Austen's novels focus on two choices: marry a rich man you don't love, or hold out for a dashing young man—who just happens to be rich. Loving a poor, ugly man did not seem to occur to Jane. Her heroines are quite interested in a man's charm and prestige, but not in his career potential. Austen novels seem to suggest that if you reject an old aristocrat, you will end up with a young aristocrat. Jane gambled and lost when she played that game.

She blamed her poverty for this predicament, but rich girls had the same basic problem. A girl with a dowry had many suitors, but that doesn't mean she got to marry for love. Fathers were not inclined to waste their money on a suitor just because he had a good body and witty repartee. Papa wanted an alliance that would raise his own status. Dowries were a way to create prominent grandchildren to carry on your legacy. If your dad chose a high-status man who was old and ugly, worse things could happen. Many girls ended up with men who gambled away their money and mistreated them. Rich girls and poor girls faced the same conundrum: Looks and charm are poor predictors of relationship skills. Today, we are free to gamble on looks and charm, but they remain poor predictors of relationship skills.

The pain that fuels Jane's work is not really about money—it's about the pain of rejection. If you are rejected by a person you "fancy," a one-down feeling surges, and cortisol makes it feel like a survival threat. In Jane Austen's time, you didn't have to face rejection yourself because your parents did the negotiating behind the scenes. Dating was taboo in Jane's time, and a girl was considered "ruined" if she expressed interest in someone who did not reciprocate. Today, we face many rejections in our mating lives, and survival-threat feelings result. If you think someone is "the one" and they reject you, it means death to your genes. You don't consciously think that, of course, so you find other threats to explain your threatened feelings.

Jane's parents dragged her to Bath to see and be seen by potential mates. Today, you can go to Bath and see the happening places of the nineteenth-century singles scene. I found it a good place to contemplate the social whirl of judging others and feeling judged by them. When you know how universal these feelings are, you can see your cortisol as a temporary internal discharge rather than external evidence of threat.

Chapter Two

Social Rivalry among Early Humans

We often hear that early humans were peaceful and egalitarian. We hear about them sharing food and bonding around the fire, so it's hard to imagine their social rivalry. This chapter presents the evidence that early humans played status games that were eerily similar to those of animals. The evidence comes from the earliest written records, and from sources that predate the invention of writing. It's clear that people have been one-upping each other since they first walked the Earth.

Ancient civilizations gave us a window into their thoughts by writing them down. Much of this writing is about social rivalry. Great leaders are always uniting followers to conquer enemies, and new leaders are always emerging by challenging the old ones. People cooperate in ancient literature when it raises their status or helps their group rise. Similar patterns are found in the writings of ancient Egypt, China, Central America, the Middle East, South America, India, Greece, and Rome.

Violence was often part of ancient status games. People were always anticipating an attack and preparing for it. Constant wariness for put-downs is a thought loop that has been reinforced since time immemorial.

The similarities between ancient civilizations and chimpanzee troops are striking. Leaders display strength, defend turf, and accumulate females. The leader shares resources with a privileged group, often descended from his many offspring. This elite group has intense status conflicts within it, but they cooperate to resist common threats to their status.

Early civilizations did something that animals do not do: They created abstract concepts to explain their superiority over foes and rivals. We call these concepts "myths" or "legends," but they were real to the people who lived with them. Animals don't create verbal rationales to justify their quest for status. Humans developed language to help us meet survival needs. Language helps us refine a plan of action and coordinate with others. Myths and legends help people coordinate their neurochemical reward systems and work together.

The belief systems of ancient civilizations were often imposed by force. Rulers inflicted severe punishment on those who questioned the prevailing cosmology. A "priesthood" designed and enforced the shared thought loops of the belief system, and thus helped rulers maintain power. Priests were richly rewarded and had top status as a result.

Ancient civilizations have a bad image today. They are accused of having destroyed the utopian world that came before them. Many academics believe that the Stone Age was peaceful and egalitarian. They zoom in on facts that fit this template and skim over facts that don't. But we know there was social rivalry in the animal world before the Stone Age, and we know there was social rivalry after the Stone Age. We know that the brain's limbic system was the same before and after. If we open our minds to the possibility of prehistoric status games, what might we find?

CRACKED SKULLS

Archeology is a good source of information about the distant past. Archeologists have been shocked by the number of human skeletons with signs of violent death. These include:

- skeletons with a stone arrow tip embedded in them;
- skulls cracked in the precise way that a blunt instrument would cause;
- piles of skeletons buried together without care;
- skulls with the top two vertebrae attached, which results from beheading;
- skeletons piled up at the gates of protective walls;
- skeletons with cutting and scraping marks, suggesting cannibalism;
- large stocks of rocks in the missile shape used in battle.

With this evidence, some archeologists have estimated the percentage of deaths attributable to violence in prehistory as quadruple the rate of a dangerous inner city today.

Archeologists ignored this evidence at first because they were convinced that prehistoric humans were peaceful. They looked for other interpretations when they found the artifacts listed above. They were rewarded with academic status if they conformed to the empathy-around-the-fire view of human origins. If they acknowledged prehistoric violence, they were denigrated and ostracized. Despite the significant career risk, evidence of Stone Age social rivalry accumulated.

Nonviolent competition is also apparent in the archaeological record. Ancient skulls in South America show that people flattened the foreheads of their children with pressure devices in order to create a desired appearance. Parents saw the flat foreheads of their neighbor's children and didn't want their kids to fall behind.

Another indicator of prehistoric conflict is the dispersion of people around the globe. At a time when the Earth's population was a tiny fraction of what it is today, humans spread themselves into every corner of it. Scholars tell us that group bonds were the focus of life, but many people obviously left anyway. Perhaps they left in groups, fissuring as a group got too large, just as chimps do. But their strong motivation to leave is reflected in the fact that the bones of Stone Age *Homo sapiens* are found throughout the planet.

The urge to leave is easy to understand from an animal perspective. Mammals cluster when predators lurk and spread out when it's safe. Tigers and orangutans are the only mammals with no predators, and the only mammals who live alone. Gibbons space themselves out in pairs to prevent conflict. It's easy to see how humans would try to avoid conflict by spacing themselves out. Not only does it improve access to resources, but it frees you from being at the bottom of the hierarchy. If you persuade others to leave with you, you are suddenly in the one-up position. Some people surely perished when they left their natal groups, but others went on to create new settlements that would fissure themselves in time. Leaving is an effective way to raise your status when you don't expect to win a direct conflict.

Apart from migration, premodern people rarely left their village in a lifetime because the risk of getting killed by strangers was so high. Today, we rub shoulders with strangers in safety all the time and don't appreciate what an achievement this is. But when we shake hands, we echo the old custom of proving that you don't have a rock hidden in your hand. We like to imagine early humans with a peace pipe, but they had a lot of conflict.

TROUBLE IN PARADISE

Another way to learn about early humans is to talk to living people from ancient cultures. Today, that's hard to do, but in the past three centuries, many indigenous groups were studied at length. It's easy to criticize these studies, yet they provide a wealth of information about the human core.

I've always been interested in early contacts with isolated groups, and when I had a chance to go to Tahiti, my interest grew. I had heard that the first European ships to arrive there were greeted by Tahitian girls rowing out to offer their bodies. I wanted to know the truth of that story.

Step one of my research was easy: The story is true. It was corroborated by many sources, though expressed euphemistically due to the sensibilities of the past. But I wanted to know what motivated the girls. I knew the sexual-liberation explanation offered by anthropologists like Margaret Mead, but I wondered if that was the whole story.

It was not. It is clear from the published journals of eyewitnesses that the girls were compensated with an iron nail. Metal did not exist on Tahiti, and the girls' fathers and brothers were eager to get it. The first British ship to visit Tahiti lost so many nails that it began to fall apart. It returned to London just before Captain Cook's first voyage. Cook met the returning captain and determined to prevent such "contact." But just in case, he loaded extra nails.

I spent my life in academia, so I know it's taboo to acknowledge facts that reflect badly on indigenous cultures. But when I retired from academia, I gave myself permission to follow the facts instead of pleasing critics. I wanted to understand a culture that sold its daughters and sisters to aliens.

I learned that Tahitian girls were taught to please men from a young age. The death penalty is attached to a long list of behaviors in Tahitian culture. These are called "taboo" in the Tahitian language, which is the origin of our word. Women eating with men was one taboo. Even men could be put to death for allowing women to eat in their presence. I could imagine the culture of fear that prevailed in a society with such strictures. I would not call it "sexual liberation" when that society sent girls to get nails for their fathers and brothers. I would call it submission.

Idealized images of Polynesia have been popular for a long time. Paul Gauguin's paintings of Tahitian women have been popular since the 1800s. I started wondering about the girls in those paintings. I found out that the aging Gauguin lived with a teenager whose mother arranged the association in hopes of raising the family's status. When we see images of preindustrial societies, we presume they are happier because we don't see the signals that trigger our own unhappiness. We know our own status frustrations, but we don't know theirs. Gauguin's paintings represent the dream that you can escape status games by going somewhere else. The fact is that Gauguin drank himself to death in Polynesia while striving to become famous in Europe. Sexually transmitted disease sped the process.

Tahitians came from a seafaring culture that spread throughout the Pacific. When you visit Hawaii, you encounter many of the same cultural patterns. One of the first Hawaiians to become literate wrote a book on their ancient traditions called *Hawaiian Antiquities*. He described the taboos and the chiefs who enforced them and chronicled the lavish lifestyle of the nobility. A huge portion of the oral tradition he wrote down pertained to the warfare that brought each chief to power until a new war replaced him with a new chief.

When I visit Hawaii, I see celebrations of this tradition everywhere. Symbols of Hawaiian monarchy are gushed over by people who despise monarchy elsewhere. The yellow robe that symbolizes Hawaiian chiefs is revered by people who would otherwise object to a garment made by killing thousands of birds. Revering indigenous culture raises your status among educated elites, and that feels good. Believing in a utopia feels good too. The truth about Polynesian social rivalry does not feel good. But the truth helps you understand the world and your inner world.

The Europeans who went to Tahiti were mammals too, of course. They competed with each other in world trade, and thus competed for ports to restock their ships en route. Different European countries built alliances with different Polynesian leaders. Over time, one alliance fought another. Each group believed they needed dominance to protect itself from dominance-seeking rivals.

Captain Cook's role in this story is well known, but his brilliance at status games is not. In Cook's time, sailors on long voyages often died a horrible death of scurvy. He looked for a solution and heard that no one got sick on ships serving sauerkraut. The reason was unknown, but he loaded up sauerkraut. His sailors refused to eat it, alas, so he devised a clever strategy. He put large platters of the Vitamin-C-rich concoction on the officers' table and gave his sailors unprecedented permission to help themselves from it. Suddenly there was huge demand, and no scurvy ever appeared on Cook's ships. (Citrus fruit replaced sauerkraut in time.) Cook died in a conflict on the shores of Hawaii, and his story reminds me that dominant chimpanzees rarely die of old age.

Let's sail away from Polynesia and look at other sources of information about early human status games.

IT'S STILL THE SAME OLD STORY

Oral tradition can tell us a lot about our distant ancestors. When humans invented writing, they wrote down tales that were already being told. Famous examples include Homer's *Odyssey*, the Upanishads, and even the Bible. These tales revolve around social rivalry. They suggest a life full of conflict, revenge, and supreme leaders striving to display their power. The status games of high-ranking nobles and priests play a big part in oral tradition too.

We tend to learn about these ancient tales through teachers and the media rather than directly, and thus see them through a specific lens. A teacher can extract a line about peace from a war saga and create the impression that the ancients were focused on peace. A journalist can refer to compassion in the ancient world and ignore the gory cruelty that prevailed. The point is not that we should focus on gore; it's that we need to understand our deeper impulses in order to manage them. When our thought leaders idealize the past, it reinforces the message that "our society" is the source of all woes. When your information is filtered to fit this belief, it's hard to see the rest of the story.

Such filtering is especially marked in anthropology. A century ago, anthropologists spread around the world to record the traditions of people with no written language. They created a record that fits the academic mindset. An anthropologist must present other cultures in a positive light in order to get respect from other anthropologists. If they suggest that other cultures are actually superior to ours, they get extra status. Thus, we end up with a lot of messaging about cooperation, altruism, and female power in preliterate societies. That would be good if it were true, but a different picture emerges when you look beyond academic sources.

One alternative source is the journals of explorers and missionaries who spent time with preliterate peoples in past centuries. These sources are often condemned as "racist" and "imperialist," so you risk being so labeled yourself if you read them. Yet there are a lot of them, and they have much in common. They portray a world of brutal violence toward out-groups, and in-groups surging with jealousy, competition, and vengeance.

Nonconforming anthropologists are another good source of information. They have reported status hierarchies and a fervent quest for prestige in many hunter-gatherer societies. They have found high levels of violence, and cultures that focused on preparing for battle. Examples include long-term research among the Amazon's Yanomamo and the highland tribes of New Guinea. Researchers found that about 25 percent of males died in violent conflict—a rate equivalent to Jane Goodall's estimate of violent deaths among chimpanzees. In New Guinea, dozens of mutually unintelligible languages exist in a small area. This is evidence of minimal communication between neighboring groups. Abuse of women was also widely in evidence.

Most important, researchers found that men who distinguished themselves in battle had more wives and more surviving offspring. Today, we do not measure status by the number of children one has, nor do we think of violence as a high-status activity. But in the past, success in battle was the main way for a male to raise his status. Once you achieved that status, your access to resources improved, and thus your reproductive success improved. You may have died young, but your genes were more likely to survive. The result is a culture that glorifies success in battle and prepares children for it at an early age.

These battles were not wars the way we think of them today. They were brief raids against neighboring groups. They happened quite often, as each group sought to revenge a past raid or forestall a future raid. Few people died in each raid, but, cumulatively, they killed a large share of the population. Children grew up learning about wrongs done to their ancestors, and the cycle continued. Chimpanzees raid their neighbors in a remarkably similar way.

GIFT GIVING

Nonviolent ways to raise your status are valuable, and in ancient societies, gift giving was a key way to do that. Group leaders often presented huge gifts to the leaders of neighboring groups. Scholars may call such gifts "sharing" or "altruism," but weaker leaders gifted stronger leaders to avoid being raided. Gifts were also used to curry favor with a leader to gain access to their resources. Gifts flowed down the status hierarchy too, as leaders tried to buy support in the face of rivals.

Gifts took many forms, from commodities to precious creations to your daughter. Banquets were a common form of gifting. People competed for dominance by giving bigger banquets. Today, these banquets are represented as a way to feed the poor. This benevolent view overlooks the way leaders got the food—often from those they were ostensibly feeding.

Ancient gift-giving rituals are curiously similar to the grooming behavior of monkeys. Research has shown that monkeys make careful decisions about which members of their group to groom. Sometimes they groom stronger individuals who might protect them in times of threat. Sometimes they groom weaker individuals who might side with them during conflicts. The expected reciprocity doesn't always happen, alas. A monkey who counts on an alliance may be disappointed when a threat appears. Monkeys start grooming new partners if they survive such betrayed expectations.

The reciprocal nature of grooming is famously portrayed in the opening scene of *The Godfather*. A man offers gift money to the Godfather in hopes of buying vengeance on an enemy. The Godfather refuses the money, suggesting that he must be groomed regularly rather than just patronized on a fee-for-service basis. The Godfather doesn't accept gifts from just anyone. You have to join his alliance with repeated gift giving in order to share in his power.

Acknowledging the reciprocity of gift giving is taboo in polite society, but the mammal brain is good at calculating return on investment. Your verbal brain represents gifts as spontaneous expressions of generosity, and it's taboo to verbalize your reciprocal expectations. The rituals of gift giving in early human cultures help us understand our deeper longings. Gifts to the gods are an especially interesting example.

HIGH PRIESTS

In ancient civilizations, high priests told people the right way to offer gifts to the gods. It seemed like a matter of life and death because the gods were believed to control the weather, disease, and warfare. With so much at stake, you were eager to know how to please the gods, and high priests were eager to tell you. It didn't always work, but priests had top status, so you tended to believe them.

You wanted to offer the best gift you could afford, and you also wanted the best priest, shaman, or soothsayer you could afford. Sometimes, they insisted on huge gifts, including human sacrifice. It's useful to think about why people went along with this. Our brain is designed to anticipate harm, and we are highly motivated to prevent it. We're not sure what works, so we look for clues. When others assert confidence in their own solutions, and we see them get respect, trusting them meets our need to feel safe. When priests are wrong, you could blame yourself for failing to do enough of whatever they proposed.

Leaders fear threats just like others, so they often rely on a priesthood. Most ancient cultures had a priestly class at the top of the status hierarchy. Priests gained power through their influence over top leaders. In many places, they could have you tortured and killed if you didn't submit to them.

Being a priest was a coveted position, so the price of admission was high: You had to submit completely to the reigning priesthood. As a result, priests may appear to have high status, but they must live in complete submission to maintain that status.

The main threat to a priest's status was competition from another priesthood. If new priests prevented harm more successfully, the old priesthood suffered. Thus, we often see high priests banding together to condemn a rival priesthood. Nasty conflict between rival priests played a huge role in human history.

In today's world, academics and the media are quite similar to ancient priesthoods. They tell us how to manage potential threats, and how to give gifts in a way that makes us right with the world. Their status is high, and top leaders rely on them. If you want to share in their status, you have to submit to their dogma. Fortunately, their power is more limited than in the past. We can choose which priests we respect in our quest to feel safe. This freedom of choice intensifies the rivalry among competing priesthoods.

THE STATUS GAMES OF SIGMUND FREUD

I was excited to learn that Freud's Vienna apartment is open to the public. You can see the couch where psychoanalysis began, and the toilet where he developed the anal-retention theory. You can walk to the cafe where he read his daily newspaper. It was a moving experience for me.

I didn't love Freud when I did this. I disagreed with many of his assertions, and I'd learned to see him as a shady character. But in time, I learned to reference my internal sense of truth instead of relying on high priests to define it. Then I recognized Freud's contribution. He showed us that our thoughts have power. He helped us recognize our unbidden nonverbal thoughts and build our power to redirect them. He played some unpleasant status games while he spread this idea. He made some bad calls because he was wired by past experience. But without him, we might still believe the lies we tell ourselves.

Freud's status games were fascinating because he was both at the top of the hierarchy and at the bottom. He saw himself at the top spot because he was his mother's favorite. She openly favored him in front of her five other children, and she expected him to make it big. Young Freud was always at the top of his class in school despite coming from a low-status family. In college, he got internships with high-profile researchers and was mentored by

Vienna's most prominent doctor. This mentorship included cash "loans," as well as access to the cigar box and even the bathtub (a luxury at the time) of the eminent Dr. Josef Breuer. He was also invited to tag along when Dr. Breuer treated patients by asking them about their feelings. Freud's status was ultimately crowned by many best-selling books and by disciples flocking in from around the world for treatment and training.

But Freud's bottom-of-the-barrel experiences were huge, and foremost in his mind. In school, he was surrounded by the super-rich while he often lacked money for the barest food and clothing. His classmates saw him as a pretentious twit, and perhaps he was. In college, he was always desperate for money, but he couldn't spend any he got without first helping his hungry family.

Most important from the perspective of evolutionary psychology, his sex life was quite deprived. In an era without birth control, respectable women were unavailable until you could support the children who quickly came along. Other women were likely to have venereal diseases, which were incurable then. It appears that Freud had no sexual relations until he was thirty. Then, after ten years of almost constant pregnancy, he went back to total abstinence. (Accounts vary.) But that was not the problem that concerned him, consciously. He was preoccupied by the problem of making a name for himself.

Freud dreamed of making a breakthrough in medicine. It's easy to see why that would interest him. The germ theory of disease was revolutionizing medicine in his time, and he lived at the center of the action. The hospital he worked at was the site of the famous study about doctors washing their hands to prevent deaths from "childbed fever." That study was ridiculed and sneered at for years, but by Freud's time, acceptance had grown. The subject would have caught Freud's attention because Freud's father lost his first wife at a young age.

Freud's first job in laboratory research paid about as much as the janitor. He would never have sex if he stayed there. He stumbled onto the idea of treating rich people with nervous disorders. At first, he used treatments that were popular in his day, but in time he gravitated toward the "talking cure." The more talk he heard, the more he concluded that sex was at the root of mental health problems.

The story gets murky here, since we can't be sure what his patients said and what he projected onto them. But Freud announced to the world that "infantile sexuality" was the cause of emotional distress. He was shunned by the medical establishment, but his books became popular. People seemed eager for an explanation of human irrationality.

The wrongheadedness of his theory of infantile sexuality should not distract us from its valuable underpinnings: that childhood and sex play a huge role in our emotions. Freud erred by putting these factors together and saying that children are motivated by sex. But the two ideas separately have revolutionary value. They seem obvious today because people have worked to establish them.

Why did Freud go too far and insist on such a wacky theory? It made me wonder what was going on in *his* childhood. I went digging for that.

Freud revealed little of his actual history, despite his endless psychoanalyzing of himself in the abstract. He revealed more in letters, but some of those letters are still in sealed archives today. Fortunately, a lot of information has been compiled by eager researchers.

Freud's father had children from an earlier marriage who were the same age as Freud's mother. One of those children had a family already, so Freud grew up hearing his father called "grandpa." For a time, little Sigi thought his half-brother was his father and his father was his grandfather.

He was confused about his mother too, because she left him with a nurse most of the time. The nurse was suddenly banished when he was three, which would have been traumatic since she was his primary attachment. She had already traumatized him with her frequent talk about burning in hell. Freud later blamed his trauma on the fact that she touched his genitals when she bathed him. It's easy to see how his brain would have built a link between her and genitalia, and another link between her and trauma. These links were with him when he listened to his patients' traumas. So he didn't get everything right. The pioneer doesn't get everything right in most areas of human inquiry. Even Isaac Newton thought he could turn lead into gold.

In Freud's letters, he expresses a deep sense of shame. Children often feel shame when something is wrong in their home, even though it's not their fault. Much was wrong in Freud's home. His mother seems to have been quite close to one of his grown stepbrothers. That young man suddenly fled the country and appears to have made a living from financial fraud. Freud's father seems to have participated in the fraud, which would explain why the father of six had no known employment. The family had a middle-class life for a short time, and then had no income except what they begged from relatives. They lived in tight quarters, which helps a boy wonder what Daddy is doing to Mommy. But that was not the real trauma, despite all of Freud's theorizing about it. It seems that young Sigi noticed that his family was different, so he idealized it, and then buried his head in books.

Freud was still living with his parents at age twenty-seven, even though he'd finished medical school years earlier. This was more normal at the time, of course. Young people rarely moved out until they were ready to support a family, and helped support their parents until then. But Freud was mama's golden boy (literally, she called him that), so he was allowed to pursue his dream instead of supporting them.

Freud's medical internship was mind-boggling. He learned to diagnose patients in the psychiatric ward and then autopsy their brain if they died. His supervisors believed that mental illness always had a physical cause. They were sure the cure would come if they kept dissecting brains. But Freud needed money fast, so he quit the low-paying work that he loved and hung out his own shingle. His talking cure soon found paying customers, and it opened his mind to the idea that our thoughts can affect our body. He worked to spread this insight to others, and for that I applaud him.

Freud spread his ideas by building social alliances. But the record shows that many of his friends became enemies over time. He'd build close bonds with a new friend, only to end up with another enemy. It's easy to find fault with him, but if he had gone along with whatever was popular, we might not have our current awareness of our unconscious. Many of Freud's "enemies" started their own therapeutic approaches, which spread his valuable insights without the baggage of infantile sexuality.

Criticizing Freud is popular, and I joined in the sneering myself when I was young. But after reading psychology for decades, I have seen many paradigms come and go. Each new paradigm vilifies the one that came before it. Freud was vilified by behaviorists, who were themselves vilified by later psychology paradigms, such as cognitive, genetic, evolutionary, social justice, and positive psychology. Vilification is a status game. It masquerades as "science," but each paradigm is a social alliance that sifts facts in a way that raises the status of that alliance. I have learned to pick the best from each paradigm instead of taking any one of them as "fact." I could not do that if I were gainfully employed in the psychology world, since my credentials would depend on submitting to the high priests of that alliance. Retirement has freed me to connect the dots for myself.

We all draw our own conclusions about how the mind works because our mammal brain cannot talk to us in words. A great place to ponder your own brain is on Freud's favorite walking path in the Vienna Woods. It's called the "Beethoven Way" because it's the very path that Beethoven walked while composing in his head. You can analyze yourself on a walk through the Vienna Woods the way Freud did. You can discover the circuits you built from early experience. If it leads to a catharsis, you can thank Freud for that concept.

Freud moved to London when the Nazis took Vienna, and I visited his London home too. He managed to ship his new couch and his antiquities there, so you can see the little statues from ancient civilizations that flooded his office. To him, these statues were evidence of the ageless human grappling with the unconscious mind.

Chapter Three

Status Games around the World

Cultures vary on the surface, but underneath they have similar status games.

The cultural diversity we see on the outside distracts us from the common mammalian thought loops we have on the inside.

We often blame our culture for the frustrations of social rivalry and imagine that other cultures have effortless happiness. So it's helpful to know that other cultures have the same frustrations. All over the world, people are trying to one-up each other and feeling bad about being one-down. These behaviors might be explicit, like kowtowing to the emperor in Imperial China, or the caste system in India, or the aristocracy in Europe and Japan. But they can also be subtle, so you don't see them as a status game. Wearing blue jeans is a good example.

Blue jeans began as work clothes, but they acquired status in the mid-twentieth century as symbols of rebellion. Rebelling puts you in the one-up position, at least in your own mind. Rebelling allows young people to feel superior to their parents who paid for the jeans. Most wearers of blue jeans are not actually rebelling, of course. On the contrary, they are conforming. But conforming to a symbol of rebellion allows you to feel one-up while you get on with the business of getting along with your fellow mammal. It says you are not submitting to "the man." This makes it a safe way to oppose stronger individuals, from your mammal brain's perspective. When you see others wearing jeans, you feel like you're part of a strong alliance. Blue jeans can give your inner mammal the sense of strength that it longs for.

Many other status games are similar worldwide. Long before modern technology, distant lands had eerily similar status games. Here are some well-known examples, from the tangible use of clothing to the intangible quest for "honor."

COMMON THREADS

Stone Age graves show that people took pride in their bodily adornment. Clothing is central to status games in every culture because it's one of the first things you notice when you compare yourself to others. Throughout history, people have used clothing to raise their status.

In Medieval Europe and Asia, laws prescribed what you could and couldn't wear at each level of society. Even the underwear of each social class was regulated by these "sumptuary laws." Harsh penalties were attached, so you could not look like a noble just because you could afford a pouffy shirt. Everyone was forced to wear a hat that quickly identified their social rank. In China, specific hats denoted specific levels within the aristocracy, using a feather, tassel, or pompom.

Today, we'd be outraged by laws that banned haute couture from all but the rich. But if you look at these laws from the perspective of Queen Elizabeth I, you might see it differently. England's Renaissance queen knew her courtiers were spending ruinous amounts of money on their clothing. And she knew how viciously they gossiped about the appearance of other courtiers. She also knew that the "commoners" tried to mimic the fashions worn at court. The result was a fashion arms race that was bad for everyone. Elizabeth didn't want her courtiers to waste their wealth on foreign silk. She wanted them to spend it on horses to strengthen national defense. Also, she wanted her subjects to be able to visit her court without bankrupting themselves on an appropriate outfit. So she passed laws freezing in the fashions of yesterday, hoping to prevent wasteful new styles.

The law did not apply to her, of course. She constantly tried to dazzle the court with bigger fashion statements. As she got old and decrepit, she felt one-down toward the beautiful young ladies at court. How could she one-up them? It's easy to see why sumptuary laws would appeal to her.

In time, people rebelled by wearing black. Look at Rembrandt's paintings and you will see the black style of the time. Alas, the fad did not stop the fashion arms race because a white lace collar was permitted. The collar got bigger and bigger. The ruffles grew closer and closer. The embroidery grew finer and finer. These collars were crushingly expensive due to the labor necessary to maintain them as well as the delicacy of the fabric. Your ruffles had to be pressed to perfection each morning to avoid public shaming. Black dye was also quite expensive, and black fabric faded quickly. High maintenance costs are a common feature of status objects in every time and place.

Wearing black was supposed to reduce social rivalry, but the opposite happened. The black-wearing people built strong social bonds and started England's Civil War. That war is explained with sophisticated rationales, but it's easy to see how the black-robed Puritans would have felt their strength when they saw how many others wore black. You can see how their internal divisions would ease when they compared themselves to colorfully dressed people. When you see yourself as part of a strong social alliance, your inner mammal rewards you with a good feeling.

In France, fashion was also at the core of social rivalry, but in a different way. Louis XIV ruled through fashion by adopting new styles every season, and pushing the nobility to follow. No imports were allowed, and French suppliers paid heavy taxes to Louis. It was a money machine for him, but he is also credited with starting the French fashion industry. Their garments got bigger and bigger, and when physical limits were reached, Marie Antoinette extended the competition into hair. Her hairdos got bigger and bigger in order to one-up the ladies who imitated her. Once she was dispatched, people started imitating the garb of Napoleon's wife. The hardships of war descended on Europe, but they were no match for the hardship of being seen in last year's dress. Everyone suddenly had to have Josephine's "empire waist."

When I was in college, I was taught to blame this behavior on the fashion industry. We were told that greedy capitalists lure people to waste their money on "conspicuous consumption." We were told that the advertising industry creates desire to keep up. I believed this message because it was repeated so often by teachers I looked up to. I learned to blame unhappiness on "our society," so I looked to other societies for happiness.

I got a job in Africa after graduating and was shocked to hear about conspicuous consumption from my African office mate. He complained that no one dated in his country because the bride price was higher than anyone could afford. He listed the items he had to give a girl's parents before he could talk to her: a dozen dresses, a dozen pairs of shoes, a refrigerator, pots and pans, and many other items that I've forgotten. I wondered how a society could continue if no one dated. It seems that multiple wives were permissible, so parents who held out for a high bride price would not deprive themselves of grandchildren. This fits the mammalian pattern of a few males getting a lot of reproductive success while others get none.

When I returned from Africa, I got a job at a Japanese company. There I learned that designer labels were extremely popular in Japan. It was the 1970s, and young Japanese women suddenly earned good money as "office ladies." They tended to live with their parents, so they had a lot of spending money. Extravagant luxury brands suddenly became widespread. You may blame this on "our society" in one way or another, so it's important to know that Japan had strict sumptuary laws in the Elizabethan age though it had no direct contact with England. Humans in every society manifest this urge to keep up. Look at a painting from any time or place, and you will see that everyone in the painting is dressed alike. Styles change, but everyone seems to get the memo, down to the details of their hair and accessories.

It's easy to ridicule other people's fashion trends. Holes in blue jeans are easy for me to ridicule, as each year's holes got more daring. It's hard to explain the high price tag on ripped jeans, but it's easy to explain the one-down feeling of outdated clothing. You may find yourself conforming to a trend in your world rather than living with that one-down feeling. You may resent others for judging you without noticing that you are judging too.

Today, the richest people in the world dress in a way that's quite similar to everyone else. Mark Zuckerberg's hoodie is much like yours, as are Bill Gates's sneakers. The differences are so slight that only experts can detect them. Is it worth getting upset about tiny differences when you enjoy comfort and safety beyond anything in human history? Apparently so, because many people do.

In the modern world of mass production, clothing is cheap, but the muscles underneath it are hard to come by. Muscles are the new status marker, and modern clothing is designed to show off your muscles. People who say they don't care about fashion are often quite competitive about muscles. The status value of muscles was low in the world before machines because everyone had them, but in today's sedentary world, they reflect a big investment of time, effort, and self-discipline.

HONOR AND DISHONOR

Honor is intangible, yet people strive for honor as eagerly as they seek other status markers. The human cortex can keep score with intangibles the way it does with real assets. We define honor in different ways with our verbal brains, but our mammal brains enjoy the same one-up feeling when we have it. And we suffer from the same survival-threat feelings when we think our honor is threatened. Such strong feelings about an intangible are hard to make sense of until you know that the mammal brain sees social status as a matter of survival.

Another culture's definition of honor may be easy to notice because you learn about it with your verbal brain. Your own culture's definition of honor can be hard to notice because you wired it in from youthful interactions with the people around you. Thus, it's useful to look at definitions from a wide range of cultures.

Many languages around the world have social rankings built into them. For example, when you speak Spanish, French, Chinese, or Japanese, you have to designate the person you are speaking with as either above you or below you. When I speak a foreign language, I'm uncomfortable about making these distinctions; but if I had grown up speaking one of those languages, I would do it so automatically that I would hardly notice. Native speakers know how to put themselves above or below with hardly a second thought.

Some cultures teach their children that honor is the most important thing in life. Others teach their children not to make a big deal of what others think of you. Some cultures have a big vocabulary associated with honor, while others don't talk about it. The general concepts of "reputation" and "saving face" can help us access the common feelings beneath these differences. In some cultures, you are considered "egotistical" if you worry about "losing face." In others, you are considered crazy if you don't worry about "face." You learn that dishonor must be repaired at all costs, up to and including suicide and murder. Early experience builds the circuits linking honor to survival. Your mirror neurons pick up other people's fear of dishonor, and repetition builds the pathway.

The fear of dishonor has real roots. Being ostracized from society can have serious consequences. Maybe you will be deprived of your livelihood. Maybe you will die alone in the desert. Maybe your genes will be wiped out because no one will mate with you. People fear these consequences, so they strive constantly for honor to relieve those fears. The fear of social ostracism motivates people to strive constantly for honor.

In some cultures, suicide is the accepted way to restore honor. The thought of achieving honor after you're gone is a big enough reward to outweigh the thought of death. Logically this doesn't make sense, but when the thought of suicide relieves your one-down feelings, it promotes survival from your mammal brain's perspective.

In today's world, people often pride themselves on discarding old traditions, but they substitute new honor codes for old ones. You risk severe sanction if you fail to honor a new norm, so people submit quickly to protect themselves. People compete to impose new norms in order to control who is honored and who is dishonored.

Some "honor codes" are explicit. The Mafia code of honor is well known for its emphasis on silence and its life-and-death consequences. The "Gentleman's Code of Honor" was the rule book for dueling in past centuries. Dueling seems foolish today, but it was useful at the time because people erupted into violence without consulting a rule book when they felt dishonored. The Samurai code of honor has been glorified in the media, but it was gory in reality. The custom of bowing began as a way of presenting your neck to your superior for them to chop with their sword if they chose. The brute force in so many honor codes is eerily parallel to the status games of animals.

An extreme code of honor is the ancient Albanian Kanun, which requires you to kill a relative of anyone who killed one of your relatives. Such "vendettas" and "blood feuds" have existed in many cultures. They have claimed a significant percentage of some populations, and terrorized everyone else. Such revenge cycles happen when people believe that a retaliatory murder will raise their status, and they'll be shamed and shunned if they don't commit it. In Albanian culture, this belief is reinforced with a custom called "coffee under the knee." If a person fails to avenge his family honor, their coffee is served to them under the table rather than on it at public events. Small shaming gestures are enough to perpetuate a cycle of violence that's deeply wired in.

Many universities have an "honor code," but that usually means self-policing. This makes it easier to cheat. I saw a lot of cheating in my twenty-five years as a college professor. I discussed this with my colleagues, and most objected to enforcement, saying, "I'm not a policeman." But I would not like cheating among surgeons or pilots or architects, so I held my classroom to the same standard I expect of others. In doing so, I effectively violated my colleagues' implied code.

"Honor among thieves" is not a formal code but it's a well-known concept. It emerges organically because people who break the law fear reporting to authorities when they are victims of a crime. This is glorified as "honor," though it is obviously self-interest. Movies create the impression that thieves have superior social bonds and that criminals are great buddies and lovers. In reality, predatory behavior tends to spread where the law is not respected.

In every subculture, people fear losing honor as defined by those around them. And in every subculture, defending the honor of others is a popular way to raise your status. Politicians compete by appealing to one-down feelings and promising to raise your status. Mass media and religions do the same, because appealing to underdog feelings is such an effective way to win support. Chinese mythology even has a special deity for people who feel wrongfully deprived of honor. According to legend, Zhong Kui got a high score on the imperial examination, but the emperor refused to give him his due because he was ugly. Zhong Kui killed himself, and when he arrived in hell, he was honored at last. He was placed at the top of the dominance hierarchy of hell, and thus became the spirit you pray to when demons are after you.

Today we are free of much traditional tribalism, and we are free to choose our own beliefs. Yet we tend to reproduce the same old underdog feelings. For example, television series with an upstairs-downstairs theme are quite popular. They lure you to feel the pleasure of wearing a sequined gown to dinner, and then they prompt you to hate that jeweled person and identify with the more honorable servants. You practically feel the chill of their dank basement even as you sit on your snug couch. A good script manipulates your emotions, so you feel the pain of downstairs ancestors that you didn't know you had. The mammal brain's focus on social comparison keeps us riveted.

I'M OFFENDED

Taking offense is a popular status game. You accuse someone of putting you down, although you are actually putting them down by accusing them. Today, it's easy to get the one-up position by being offended because you don't need proof to back your accusation—your claim that your feelings are hurt is enough. If anyone challenges that, you can accuse them of offending you too. This works if you have a social alliance big enough to cause fear in the people you accuse of offending.

When a mammal sees that an adversary has a stronger alliance, they are quickly intimidated into one-downing themselves. People scramble to build large alliances as a result. But it's a two-edged sword: If you want support in your own conflicts, you have to support others in their conflicts. You end up with a lot of conflict. If you don't play the game, you feel like an isolated gazelle in a world full of lions, or the weakest monkey at the bottom of the hierarchy. It's not surprising that many people choose to play the game. It feels good when they're in the one-up position, accusing others of giving offense and then watching them kowtow.

As frustrating as this is, it was worse in the past. You might have offended a monarch, who'd accuse you of "treason" and have you tortured and executed. You might be challenged to a duel by a person who claims to be offended. You could be murdered by relatives of someone your grandfather murdered. It's not easy being mammal, so we often submit to our culture's rule book to survive.

BUREAUCRATIC STATUS GAMES

It's easy to feel one-down when you are dealing with a government office. And it's easy to come up with greater-good arguments when your grievance is really based on self-interest. I once worked in a country where it was routine for the police to pull over a car for no reason and for the driver to hand over cash in order to be on their way. When I borrowed a friend's car one day, he advised me to honor that custom in order to stay out of trouble. I agreed, but when the time came, I was so nervous and uncool that I scared the policeman and he waved me off.

My coworkers told me that bribery was ubiquitous in countries they'd been assigned to. People bribed to get electric service and phone service, and to get their mail at the post office. They bribed to get a birth certificate, a death certificate, or a marriage license. They bribed for a driver's license, sometimes without taking the test. Teachers and doctors took bribes. And this was just retail corruption. At the top, a huge percentage of the public budget was siphoned into secret bank accounts.

As jarring as this was, it was worse to hear people justify it. They were quick to blame others for the bribes they paid and received. People seemed to take pride in their bribery skills, as if they were making charitable contributions. They ignored the way bribery hurts everyone by perverting the function a bureaucracy was meant to fill. Roads don't get built. Traffic doesn't flow safely. Chaos reigns when rules are not enforced.

Of course it feels very one-down to stand in front of a government employee. It's easy to blame the system. But none of us is an unbiased judge of the system. When you get a parking ticket, you may feel very grieved; but when you find a parking spot, you don't thank the system for making the spot available. If you get cited for running a stop sign, you may have a grave sense of injustice; but when you see someone else run a stop light, you are outraged and want them to be stopped. The verbal brain uses words like "fairness" and "justice" but defines them in terms of its self-interested survival needs.

It's hard to manage the mammalian urge to put one's self above the law, so human groups have tried endless ways to do that. Early Catholic popes prohibited priests from marrying in order to prevent them from feathering their own nest. In Asia, eunuchs were created for the same purpose. In ancient China, the Confucian examination system was designed to base government jobs on merit rather than connections. But that did not stop influence peddling. Families would pool their money to support one child through long years of study and expect the student to kick back rewards once they got into the bureaucracy. None of these strategies solved the problem of human mammals putting themselves above the law.

CHANGE

In chapter 1, we saw that chickens erupt with violence when their group size grows beyond the bird brain's ability to remember which flock mates to submit to.

Herd animals erupt with violence when they lose their leader. The fighting continues until each herd mate fights each other once, and then a new hierarchy emerges.

Humans have also embraced violence to "change the system," but the new system is often weirdly similar to the old one. My teachers talked a lot about revolutions, but they didn't talk much about the aftermath. When I read history for myself, I was stunned to learn that the English beheaded a king and then invited back his son. (And he said yes!) The French Revolution was followed by a long period of everyone fighting everyone else, and then a return to a dictator and his relatives. I was shocked to learn that France was run by the dictator's nephew fifty years after the Revolution. I wanted to hate that guy but was again surprised to learn that he did a lot of good. (He designed the Paris architecture that we admire today, and made it safe to drink the water.) Communist revolutions have fit this pattern. They've unleashed enormous violence, only to end up with regimes that suppressed rivals with cruelty similar to what came before. My "good education" trained me to see revolutionaries as the good guys, but when I learned the facts, I let go of simplistic good-guy/bad-guy schemas.

In every time and place, people have compared themselves to others and had strong feelings about their relative position. When I was young, I often heard my parents express strong feelings about status. I saw how they made assumptions about the judgments of others, and made themselves miserable over it. I vowed to change that in my own life. I thought education would help, since education is often seen as a way to free ourselves from old norms. But when I got to college, I was surprised to hear my professors express the same kind of one-down feelings that my parents had. I couldn't understand their grievances because they seemed like the top of the hierarchy to me.

My professors didn't see it that way. They saw a world in which athletes and business leaders got more respect than they did. They bitterly resented this. They'd been at the top of their classes in school, so they could not abide a world that didn't put them on top. The adult world has many different hierarchies. We can celebrate our freedom to choose the ones we frequent, or we can denigrate the ones that don't put us on top. Of course, it's not polite to admit that you hate all hierarchies except the one that you can be at the top of. You learn to find greater-good arguments to justify the hierarchy that works for you.

My professors taught me to criticize the system. I was trained to look for systemic wrongs and find evidence to support that conclusion. Many students have figured out that you can get a good grade by condemning the system whether or not you have done your coursework. Many students do not do their work, since the brain is attuned to short-run rewards. Thus, they do not develop the skills one expects from education and must rely more heavily on their skill at condemning the system.

I was trained to condemn the system when I was in school, but the message never rang true to me. My grandfather grew up in a Sicilian village where electricity and hot running water were virtually nonexistent. Dirt floors and illiteracy were common. Few people could buy shoes or meat. Most children had worms. When people made money, the Mafia took a chunk of it. Such a life was common in much of the world until the 1950s, in both western and non-western countries.

My grandfather left his village in 1910 at age sixteen, with only his eighteen-year-old brother, to work in Ohio coal mines. They made their way to Brooklyn, where hardly anyone had electricity, indoor plumbing, or a telephone by 1920. Yet, when I was born in the 1950s, these luxuries and many others were taken for granted. Yet twenty years later, my teachers saw the system that created this as an evil that must be changed. I wanted to agree because that view raises your status, but it never felt true.

In diverse cultures all over the world, people are being taught to blame their frustrations on "the system." For a long time, I didn't notice this culture of criticism, the way a fish doesn't notice water. But small experiences slowly got my attention. One happened on my internship in Haiti, when I was invited to a picnic at a dam. I wondered why people would picnic at a dam, because I had been trained to condemn dams as a blight on the landscape. She explained that Haitians lacked electricity before the new dam, so they see it as something to celebrate. That helped to open my eyes.

Condemning the system puts you in the one-up position, so your brain rewards you with serotonin. When the serotonin runs out, you want more, so you condemn the system again. To understand this thought loop, we need to understand our serotonin system.

THE STATUS GAMES OF BOOKER T. WASHINGTON

In the early twentieth century, Booker T. Washington noticed the flood of European immigrants into the United States. He started wondering what life was like where they had come from, so he went to study conditions in their homelands. He defined it as a search for the person with the worst life, and called the resulting book *The Man Farthest Down*. I was fascinated by that book, so I was eager to visit BTW's home at the Tuskegee Institute.

You may be wondering where he chose as "farthest down," so I'll start by reporting that it was my grandfather's island of Sicily. The book asserts that the poorest ex-slave in Alabama is far better off than the Sicilian farm worker. Washington went into the mines with Sicilian miners, and he knew their lives because he worked as a miner at age fourteen. He became a college president and advisor to US presidents, so I wanted to know more about him. I was thrilled to find in him the ally I'd been looking for.

Booker T. Washington was born into slavery but eagerly sought opportunities to learn to read. After emancipation, he spent a few months in school, but his stepfather pulled him out and made him work. He kept snatching a reading lesson wherever he could, reading the letters on grain sacks and stealing moments with people who could read when one came to town. His colossal efforts to get an education are described in his best-selling autobiography, *Up from Slavery*. He went on to found a college for African Americans, a teacher-training program, and a network of rural schools staffed by his former students.

Because he believed in education, Washington was frustrated when he saw it being perverted. He thought education should raise a person's productivity, but he often sensed that it was being used to raise status instead. He saw people embrace symbols of education, like reciting poetry and wearing a top hat and cane. He wanted his educational institution to teach skills with economic value to the community in addition to academic skills. The Tuskegee Institute taught twenty-seven different industrial and agricultural trades. It was so successful that new industries took root throughout the South, and famous millionaires of his era offered funding to expand the work.

But Booker T. Washington had his critics. Any mammal who becomes the center of attention is soon challenged by rivals. BTW rose to prominence with a speech he gave at the 1895 Atlanta Exposition. His speech asked Americans to focus on productivity rather than the "ornamental gewgaws of life." After the speech, he was hailed as the leading voice of African Americans. But a week later, rivals attacked him for being too cooperative with the white world. His critics were precisely the kind of people he had always seen as a detriment to education—reciters of poetry with top hats and canes. But they bonded together when they had him as a common enemy, and thus their status rose. When BTW died, his message was lost, and gewgaws seemed to gain.

I had a personal stake in this issue because I saw the same perversion of education that he saw. When I was a parent and teacher, schools had embraced "social promotion"—the policy of passing students whether or not they had mastered a skill level. Students knew they would get the reward whether or not they did the work. The brain learns from rewards, so schools that give rewards without effort train young brains to expect rewards without effort. With promotion guaranteed, education came to be seen as a burden rather than a privilege.

The terrible consequences of social promotion are widely overlooked. Such children face work above their skill set day in and day out. They learn to cover up, strategize, side-step, deflect, panic, and, alas, cheat. Teachers don't want to "judge," so little realistic feedback is available to a student. A kid can easily reach tenth grade with a third-grade reading or math level, because they stopped learning when the work exceeded their skill level.

Imagine sitting in a classroom without understanding what's going on. Imagine well-intentioned teachers and parents smiling at whatever you do instead of acknowledging the problem. Some students run from education because this is so disconcerting. Others go on to college because faking it has come to feel natural. They may not even realize that they are faking it, because they have not experienced actual mastery. They don't know what they don't know.

Booker T. Washington tackled this problem by teaching trade skills. He found that academic skills were learned more easily once a student learned how to learn in a trade program. When a student makes a chair in a carpentry class, they must grapple with reality. If the chair breaks when they sit on it, they can respond to the feedback instead of feeling judged by the chair. It takes a lot of skill to build a chair that lasts. And it takes a lot of failure to master a skill. Managing frustration is the core of all other skills. Students must learn to try again after they fail if they are to build valuable skills. They cannot do that if they are taught to see a setback as an injustice. Once the joy of learning is experienced, a person is eager to learn more. I was pleased to find that a century ago, BTW had the same frustrations with education and reached the same conclusions.

BTW arrived in Sicily around the time that my grandfather was leaving. The book describes the horrendous living conditions he found. Families lived in one room with their animals, with no lighting at all after dark. He saw barefoot women lugging heavy sacs of fruit to market, and he saw them pay the tax collector in order to enter the town. He saw child labor everywhere, from heavy portage to skilled artisanship. He saw citrus groves guarded by the Mafia, and farming tools that seemed to date from the Bible. He saw women chained together by their own relatives while they did harvest work and then being sent back to live in seclusion in mountain villages. He imagined the daughters of those women in American schools. I was fortunate to be one of those daughters, in a school that focused on productivity rather than status.

The Booker T. Washington home is a national monument that you can visit on the Tuskegee campus. It looks frozen in time, as if he just left it. When I visited, it made me happy to think that someone a century ago reached the same conclusions about focusing on your next step despite the status-seeking that swirls around you.

Part 2

HOW OUR BRAIN CREATES STATUS GAMES

Chapter Four

Serotonin and the Pleasure of Social Dominance

In polite society, it's taboo to admit that you enjoy the one-up position, so it's hard to even admit to yourself. But our brain goes there anyway, so it's important to know why. You have inherited a brain that rewards you with serotonin when you see yourself in the one-up position. Serotonin feels so good that you want to repeat behaviors that stimulated more. The good feeling is soon metabolized, alas, so we are always looking for ways to stimulate it more. Here is the evidence.

Monkey studies done in the Psychiatry Department of UCLA Medical School, and at the National Institute for Mental Health, revealed the job of serotonin in the 1970s and 1980s. One landmark study placed a one-way mirror between a group of monkeys and the "alpha" of their group. The alpha could see his troop mates, but they could not see him. He made his usual dominance gestures, but they did not respond with submission gestures because they couldn't see him. He tried again and again, puffing up his chest and thrusting his head. With each failure, his serotonin fell, and he got increasingly agitated. The experiment continued for four days, during which time his agitation grew. He needed serotonin to keep his cool, and he needed the continual submission of his group mates to keep up his serotonin.

In the late twentieth century, this body of research was reported in the *New York Times*, major medical journals, and social science textbooks. It was widely discussed in psychiatry circles. Today, it has all but disappeared. Instead, we have the disease view of serotonin, which suggests that good feelings flow effortlessly unless you have a disorder.

We learn to link serotonin to genes and the stress of "our society." Why has the rest of the story disappeared?

One reason is that animal-rights activists made violent attacks on monkey researchers in the 1990s. Lives and property were suddenly at risk. Institutions protected themselves by dropping this research except in a few high-security facilities. And researchers protected themselves by dropping any mention of studies done on laboratory animals.

A second reason for the silence is the awkwardness of the truth. If you acknowledge that social dominance feels good, people could take it the wrong way. It's safer to trust in pills.

Here is an alternative: Stop seeing yourself as a little monkey abused by bigger monkeys, and you will stop depriving yourself of serotonin. You can stimulate the good feeling without being an abusive big monkey just by trusting in your own strength. If you prefer to get serotonin from the health care system, that's your right. But habituation and side effects may send you looking for alternatives. You can discover the old pathways that trigger your little-monkey feelings, and redirect them in safe, healthy ways.

THE UNIVERSAL QUEST FOR SOCIAL DOMINANCE

In the UCLA research, the dominant male in a group of monkeys had twice the level of circulating serotonin as the others. But when he was removed from the group, another quickly took on the role, and the new guy's serotonin rose. The original alpha's serotonin dropped sharply while he was isolated. When he was returned to the group, his serotonin shot up, and his rival's serotonin fell back.

It is easy to take this the wrong way. At one extreme, you might see this as evidence that winning at any price is the path to happiness. At the other extreme, you might jump to the conclusion that others have serotonin handed to them on a silver platter while you are hopelessly deprived. Both extremes will hurt you in the long run. You can find a healthy middle ground when you have a deeper understanding of serotonin.

We have more serotonin in our digestive system than in our nervous system. This makes sense when you remember the link between food and dominance in animals. Serotonin motivates a mammal to approach food, so it's logical that serotonin would also prepare the digestive system to receive food. Even amoeba use serotonin in this way. An amoeba spends its day sampling the water around it for signs of food or threat. It moves randomly until it stumbles on a sample with food and without threat. Then it releases serotonin and moves straight ahead. Serotonin gives it the confidence to push forward—just like us!

It's essential to know that we all long for serotonin instead of thinking it's just the "alpha type." For example, when wolves lose their pack leader, another wolf steps into the role immediately. Every wolf has the capacity to lead when it sees that it is stronger than others—both females and males. When female wolves, cows, or chimps lose their dominant individual, the next strongest critter replaces her. The urge for social dominance is a survival impulse, not a personality type. Each brain seeks the good feeling in ways wired in by its past serotonin experience. This is why humans express the common drive in such diverse ways.

Asserting yourself is risky. A bad choice can eliminate a critter from the gene pool. Natural selection built a brain that alarms you with cortisol when you see the risk of conflict, so we look for safe serotonin opportunities. It may seem like there are none—that you must either bully or get bullied. But the big human cortex can make more subtle social comparisons. You can find ways to feel strong without swinging to the extremes of bullying or being bullied. Here are three simple facts about serotonin that will help you do that.

1. Serotonin Is Released in Short Spurts That Are Quickly Metabolized

Serotonin evolved to motivate us in appropriate moments. In the wrong moment, it would not promote survival. For example, if you think you're a big dog when you're not, you will make bad choices and get hurt. Your brain evolved to avoid getting hurt. It would be nice to have a proud, confident feeling every minute of every day, but our brain is not designed to give you that.

Any serotonin you manage to stimulate is soon gone. Your brain reabsorbs it and the good feeling passes. A treadmill feeling results. You always feel like you have to do more, and you see the risk that you can't make it happen. You worry that you will never feel "on top" again. When you know this is natural, it's a huge relief. You are not doing anything wrong. You are not living in a terrible world. This is just where our animal brain goes until we notice it and grab the reins.

It's hard to notice this if you accept today's popular psychology. It tells you that self-interest is bad, and happiness comes from devoting yourself to others. If that doesn't make you happy, popular psychology suggests that you have a disease, and your doctor can fix it. The disease model rests on the presumption that other people are having effortless serotonin all the time, and you are missing out. That's a very one-down feeling! Now you are even more convinced that something is wrong with you. It seems like your only choice is to bring your brain into the repair shop to have an expert work on it.

Unrealistic expectations distract us from the work of managing our natural impulses. It's more helpful to remember that everyone faces the same serotonin treadmill. They are not coasting on effortless serotonin. Our brain saves the happy chemicals for survival-relevant moments, but it defines survival in ways that don't fit the romantic view of nature. The idealized view of animals makes it harder to understand your inner mammal. The truth about animals helps you notice your impulses and redirect them.

My ability to see my inner mammal got a big boost from the "Dog Whisperer," César Millan. He worked on his grandfather's farm in Mexico, and dogs worked alongside him. He observed the difference between working dogs and pet dogs. He saw that the working dogs were calm, while pet dogs were often contentious. Millan went to Hollywood to pursue his dream of being a dog trainer, and there he saw a lot of pampered pets. He noticed how miserable and neurotic they were compared to the working dogs of his youth. Their owners were miserable too because their homes were destroyed when they left their pets alone. Powerful celebrities were dominated by their poodles until they hired César Millan.

Millan told them that dogs seek dominance. If an owner acts submissively toward their pet, the animal presumes it is the leader of the pack. Then it growls and snaps because a pack leader's job is to protect others from potential threats.

When a dog growls and snaps, the owner's response often makes things worse. Pet owners tend to discipline the animal and then hug it. This leaves the dog with the impression that it is dominant again, but also that it will be disciplined if it acts dominant. This impossible lose-lose conundrum causes the neurosis we see in pets. A dog feels safe when it has a clear sense of the hierarchy. It feels insecure when the rules change constantly. Millan taught pet owners to be consistent about their status as the pack leader.

He was attacked for this insight by advocates of the romantic view, but people with neurotic pets were thrilled to restore peace in their homes.

When I heard about this controversy, I instantly saw the relevance to parenting. I lived in a world where children were raised as pampered pets. They were often treated like the pack leader. It did not make them happy, alas. I struggled to understand what was wrong, and when I heard Millan's explanation of neurotic dogs, I understood.

People have attacked Millan's insights by suggesting that he advocates cruelty. They misrepresent the facts to justify this conclusion. Millan is often called in on emergencies: dogs who have become violent and no longer safe for families to live with. He saves the dog's life by retraining it, but the retraining has a harshness that is not his usual method. People criticize his harshness without noticing that he is putting his own life at risk with the violent dog. They want him to be "nice" to the dog, forgetting that this has already been tried. We want to believe that being nice to a mammal will make it happy, and when that doesn't work, more "nice" is the only accepted solution. Millan helped me understand why nice-ism doesn't work.

Many schools are disrupted by children who have not learned to manage their natural dominance impulse. Their families and teachers have submitted to their dominance in the past, so their brains have learned to repeat this behavior. As they get bigger, their unrestrained dominance seeking becomes a bigger threat.

Managing our dominance impulse is hard work. We need realistic feedback to meet the challenge.

Imagine a tiny poodle who barks ferociously at big dogs that pass by. Such behavior would not exist in the natural world, because pain would quickly teach that poodle to restrain its aggression. Only in the artificial world of pet owners will a tiny poodle bark with an unrealistic sense of its own power. We do not want to live in a world of constant barking, so we need a realistic view of our animal brain.

2. Neurons Connect When Serotonin Flows

Imagine that you hit a home run when you were young and got a huge round of applause. You felt great, thanks to serotonin. Your brain built connections among every neuron active at that moment. The next time you thought about hitting a home run, a bit of serotonin was released. Now you were motivated to practice because you could feel the reward.

Your brain is designed to learn from rewards. With each reward, you build the pathway that expects more reward in similar situations. A reward is anything that meets your needs. Once your physical needs are met, you focus on social needs. There are two different kinds of social needs: the acceptance of others and the respect of others. (More on this distinction in the following section.) When you get respect, serotonin paves neural pathways and motivates you to seek more respect in that particular way.

Imagine that you cooked dinner for your family when you were young and got great recognition. Serotonin built a pathway that expects cooking to make you feel good. Of course it's complicated because experience varies. Maybe your next meal was not appreciated. Maybe you got even more respect elsewhere. Your whole range of emotional experiences has built your expectations about what will feel good in the future. The chemicals of emotion are like paving on your neural pathways. Neurons fire more easily when they have fired before, which is why we all repeat ourselves. Neurons do not literally connect, since there is always a synapse, but experience strengthens synapses in a way that is commonly referred to as "connections."

You don't consciously think of the early experience when a pathway is activated. Your electricity simply flows to the on switch of that chemical. With effort, you can figure out the early experiences that wired you to expect one-up feelings from particular activities. Be sure to look for the pattern rather than just the specifics. For example, when I was young, I did a lot of arts and crafts projects. That doesn't mean I do crafts projects today. The deeper pattern is that my parents respected my projects enough to buy me materials and leave me alone to do them. I was thrilled to focus on a craft because it shut out other people's drama. In short, these projects were an escape from the one-down position. I was in charge when I did them. This built positive expectations about taking on a project where I called my own shots. (And yes, I did some crafts as an adult, but when my living space filled up, I found other ways to meet my needs.)

Whenever you feel strongly about something, look for an early experience that fits the basic pattern. We all seek status in ways that worked before.

Our pathways do not necessarily make logical sense. For example, children are often rewarded for bad behavior. No one intends to do that, but when a child rages, we're tempted to give them more attention. When a child is aggressive, we're tempted to yield to their demands. This feels good to the young brain, and the good feeling wires it to repeat the behavior that got rewarded. The pathway gets bigger each time bad behavior is rewarded.

If you got recognition when you threw spaghetti at the wall, you may find yourself with a strange urge to throw spaghetti. Each brain sees the world through the lens of the neural pathways it has. We have billions of extra neurons available to build alternative pathways, but it's hard to get electricity to flow into neurons that have not been developed by past activation. This is why we repeat ourselves despite our best intentions. It takes a big investment of energy to steer yourself into new neural pathways. When you understand this, you are more willing to invest the energy.

Mirror neurons play an important role in our nonverbal learning. We don't mirror all of the behavior around us. Mirror neurons only fire when we observe another individual experience reward or pain. They evolved to help us learn from the experience of others. If you see someone enjoy social recognition, your mirror neurons fire and jump-start the behavior it takes to enjoy that reward.

3. The Brain Habituates to the Rewards It Has

If you get the same thank-you for cooking dinner every night, it stops feeling like a reward. If a Broadway performer gets the same round of applause for every performance, they stop feeling it. It takes new recognition to really get your serotonin going. A standing ovation would thrill you. But if you didn't get a standing ovation the next night, you'd be disappointed. You might think, "What's wrong? Why don't they like me?"

This treadmill is a routine feature of the brain we've inherited. It's frustrating, so it helps to understand its purpose instead of seeing it as a moral failing. If you were an animal on the savannah, your survival would depend on your ability to smell food and predators. To do this, your brain habituates to all the usual daily smells, so it can tune in to the smells that hold important information. Today, you might love the smell of coffee roasting, but if you worked in a shop that roasted coffee every day, you would stop noticing the smell. If you live near a bad smell, you stop noticing that too. The brain is designed to find new information by filtering out old information.

New information about the respect of others has survival value. If a monkey gets groomed by the same old pal every day it doesn't react much, but an extra grooming by a new friend gets its attention. Of course, a rejection by an old friend is also important information, and threat chemicals are triggered. Our brain is always comparing new experiences to old expectations.

If you hit a home run, it feels great the first time. But if you hit a home run every day, it would stop turning you on.

If your spaghetti-throwing got the same response every time, the pleasure would fade, and you would look for other ways to trigger it.

The struggling artist is a well-known example of habituation. A tiny bit of recognition for your art feels great when you have none. You think you will be happy forever if you get recognition from a certain status figure in your community. But once you get it, the good feeling doesn't last, and you set your sights on another prestige accomplishment. You might even be offended by a form of recognition that would have thrilled you in the past. And if you reach the summit of achievement as defined by your life experience, you do not live on an endless cloud of serotonin. You live in constant fear of losing your place at the top. Every up-and-coming artist seems like a threat to your survival. You don't know why you feel this way. You didn't choose to feel this way. This is what happens when a big human cortex is plugged into a standard mammal brain.

Habituation helps your brain focus on the unmet need. If you were dying of thirst in the desert, any sign of an oasis would thrill you. But when you have unlimited running water, it does not make you happy. Our ancestors survived because they focused their energy on the unmet need. When they found a good fishing hole, they didn't celebrate forever; they looked for more resources to meet more needs. We have inherited the brain of survivors.

This is why people often feel like they have to hit more home runs or cook bigger dinners or throw more spaghetti at the wall. And of course, it's why people think the next promotion or the next romance will make them happy forever. When the good feeling fades and a threatened feeling starts, you don't know why. It's easy to blame the job, the romance, and "our society."

You may see a contradiction between habituation and expectations. There is a contradiction! Old pathways make you think something will feel good, but when you get it, it doesn't feel as good as you expected. This is the core of addiction. People "chase the first high" because their brain is so good at recording that first high. Imagine your first bite of a homemade brownie. It thrills your taste buds. It's the best brownie you've ever had. But if you have another one, it's no longer the best brownie ever. An even richer, gooier brownie would be needed to get that thrill. The pathways paved by happy chemicals become your baseline. In the future, you compare new experiences to that. If it's not better, your brain doesn't waste happy chemicals on it.

It's easy to condemn this impulse in others—and in yourself. It's useful to keep remembering its value. You would not be reading a book if your first bit of knowledge made you happy forever. I would not be writing a book if my second-grade story made me happy forever. Our brain evolved to reward us for new ways of meeting needs, not for sitting on the couch.

SEROTONIN VS. DOPAMINE, OXYTOCIN, AND ENDORPHIN

The good feeling of serotonin is different from the good feeling of dopamine, oxytocin, or endorphin. Nature gave us different reward chemicals to motivate us to meet different survival needs. We want all of them. Knowing the difference helps us understand status games.

Dopamine is the joy of meeting a need. If you are hungry and see food in the distance, your dopamine surges. You feel excited and energized to approach the reward. If your belly is full, other rewards get your attention. Your big human cortex can anticipate future threats to your resources. You look for ways to relieve potential threats, and when you find something, dopamine is your reward.

Oxytocin is the good feeling of social trust. Mammals seek safety in numbers because it promotes survival. Oxytocin is the good feeling that it's safe to lower your guard. But sticking with the herd is frustrating, and a mammal would rather wander off to greener pasture sometimes. If it did, it would quickly be picked off by predators, so natural selection built a brain that rewards you with the good feeling of oxytocin when you stick with the herd. When you're isolated, your oxytocin falls, and you start to feel unsafe. When you return to the herd, oxytocin surges. This wires you to expect a good feeling from social support.

Endorphin means "endogenous morphine." It's the body's natural opioid, triggered by real physical pain. Endorphin masks pain with a euphoric feeling, which enables an injured animal to run to save its life. Endorphin evolved for emergencies only. We are not meant to inflict pain on ourselves to get it. We are meant to seek dopamine, serotonin, and oxytocin, but not to seek endorphin. People do seek it, of course. "Runner's high" is the well-known example. Runners don't get high every time they run. They have to run to the point of pain.

Each of these chemicals has its own job to do, but they often work in combination. Let's see how they combine with serotonin. Imagine that you do a specific task in the expectation of a promotion. Serotonin creates the expectation that a promotion will feel good, and dopamine creates the excitement you feel as you take steps to approach the re-ward. Imagine that you do a good deed for your loved ones. Your brain anticipates both the oxytocin of social acceptance and the serotonin of social importance. Imagine that you're training for a marathon. Sero-tonin creates the expectation of enormous pride if you finish, which stimulates the dopamine that motivates your daily workouts, and in turn stimulates endorphin.

It would be nice to enjoy happy chemicals all the time, but our brain saves them for moments when survival action must be motivated.

Imagine a hungry monkey who sees a piece of fruit in the distance. Dopamine is triggered thanks to past experience, and the good feeling motivates pursuit. The dopamine stops as soon as the monkey gets the fruit because it has already done its job. The reward value of a piece of fruit depends on how hungry the monkey is and how scarce the fruit is. In a modern supermarket, fruit is so abundant that it doesn't excite us, but when my mother was a child, it was so scarce that she was excited when she got an orange for Christmas. The good feeling motivated my mother to take steps that enabled her to purchase more oranges in the future.

Imagine two monkeys grooming each other's fur. Touch triggers oxytocin, and it feels good. But any monkey close enough to touch you is close enough to kill you. A monkey doesn't let another get that close unless there is already trust based on past oxytocin experiences. Social trust feels good, but trusting everyone is bad for survival. The mammal brain is designed to make careful decisions about when to expect social support.

Our brain did not evolve to give you free happy chemicals all the time for no reason. It evolved to save good feelings for new action to meet your needs. Today, it's easier to fill your belly, so other needs get your attention. We have more energy to invest in the pursuit of social rewards because we are not busy foraging for food, water, and firewood. Thus, in a world that's safer than our ancestors' wildest imagining, we can end up feeling bad about small social disappointments.

PRIORITIES

Our brain is always deciding which need to focus on. We are not consciously aware of these decisions most of the time. To become aware of them, imagine you're on a camping trip, and you're hungry, cold, and exhausted. You decide which need is most urgent, and once you've met it, you decide what the next most urgent is. It takes a lot of energy just to meet your basic needs. When the camping trip is over, you go back to meeting your needs on autopilot. Now you have more energy left to meet social needs. They start to feel more pressing. You long for another camping trip. Social status feels less urgent when your energy is used up by chopping wood and finding shelter.

Your brain is designed to focus on the unmet need. When you have physical safety and social support, the urge for status gets your attention. You notice that some of your group mates get more respect than you get. When you don't get the recognition you expect, you feel one-down. The bad feeling grabs your attention when your other needs are met. You look for a way to stimulate your serotonin to relieve it. Since you don't know how your neurochemicals motivate you, your verbal brain comes up with a way to explain it.

Mammals build strength through social alliances, and humans do the same. Joining a powerful or high-status group is a fast, easy way to enjoy serotonin, and it meets your oxytocin needs too. This only works if the group accepts you, so gaining admission to powerful and prestigious groups is a popular activity. Approaching this goal stimulates dopamine. It's easy to see why so much human energy is focused on raising the status of your group.

AMBITION

Ambition is the word often used for the serotonin quest.

Ambition is both admired and condemned. People tend to applaud the ambition of potential allies, while resenting the ambition of potential rivals. This is why you may be thrilled by a brilliant athletic performance from "your team," but scowl at the same performance when a rival team does it. Your brain measures things in relation to your own one-up urges, even if you insist it's just about the skill.

Watching others score a goal feels good, but scoring your own goal feels better. You look for opportunities that you think you can score at, and as soon as you anticipate success, you enjoy a bit of serotonin.

Our big cortex is designed to anticipate. Humans plant in the spring because we anticipate relief of hunger in the fall. We sacrifice for our children because we anticipate the survival of our line. We tolerate today's cortisol because we anticipate tomorrow's serotonin.

Your ambition may get a bad reaction from your group mates. If you share your anticipation of pleasure, they may react with alarm instead. They may say they are just trying to protect you, but the fact is that you have less energy to invest in group goals when you are investing in individual goals. So their alarm is motivated by their own interest, even if they point to the greater good to justify it. All through human history, groups have discouraged individual ambition in order to promote the group's survival. This is easily done by pointing to common enemies, and by threatening individualists with expulsion.

Now you're left with a difficult choice. A popular solution to this dilemma is to seek individual recognition in the name of the greater good.

The dream of saving your group is a perennial meme of human culture. Young people have always dreamed of being the hero who rescues their group. The bigger the enemy, the bigger the hero you can be. Today's focus on "saving the world" is a new manifestation of an old thought loop. Each generation strives to rescue others from the threats perceived in their time and place. Each step toward this ambition triggers the good feeling of serotonin. But you face a lot of competition from rival rescuers of the world. You have to manage a lot of threatened feelings to get serotonin, so let's take a closer look at the threat chemical, cortisol.

THE STATUS GAMES OF SOONG CHING-LING (MADAME SUN YAT-SEN)

I visited three former residences of Soong Ching-ling on my visits to China. They gave me a thrilling "insider" feeling on history. If you haven't heard of Soong Ching-ling, you will understand her dilemma anyway because she was a mammal among mammals just like you. She was widely revered in China as the wife of its first "revolutionary," Sun Yat-sen. She lost her place on the world stage when she was widowed in her early thirties, and she urgently wanted it back. How she got it is a testament to the human urge for serotonin in the face of cortisol.

Rival factions fought over the vacuum left by the fall of China's imperial rules, and each faction was eager to have Sun Yat-sen's widow to confer legitimacy on it. She could have her pick. She chose the Communist Party over the Nationalist Party that her husband and her father had founded. Why?

Sun Yat-sen had lost control over the party before he died. Now, it welcomed Madame Sun as a symbol, but not as a player. Sun himself had allied with the Communists at the end of his life. He could not get support anywhere else after so many of his "uprisings" failed, so he took support from Moscow. The Communists were eager to support Soong Ching-ling too. She loved being in the spotlight again. She didn't say that, of course. Throughout her life, she explained every decision by invoking her love of China.

The honeymoon was over when Ching-ling realized that the Communists wanted her as a follower rather than a leader. Her male comrades submitted to Moscow and expected her to do the same. But Ching-ling was accustomed to the prima-ballerina role. Her father was one of the richest men in China, having prospered from ties to organized crime. Charlie Soong had spent time at a Bible school in the US South in his teens, and he wanted his three daughters to have the same opportunity. It was unheard of for Chinese girls to study abroad in the early twentieth century, so the Soong sisters had an unusual breadth of experience.

Ching-ling had grown up seeing Sun Yat-sen work with her father on revolutionary plans in her own living room. When she returned from college, Dad made her Sun's secretary. Sun was a huge celebrity at the time, and though he was thirty years older and married, Ching-ling responded to the overtures. Dad objected vehemently, having seen Sun mistreat the wife he already had. Ching-ling eloped, citing her love of China.

But Sun did her wrong, alas. Among other things, he endangered her life, and their unborn child's life, to save his own. Ching-ling did not want a divorce—she wanted to be a player. From then on, she insisted on accompanying her husband to all political meetings and appearances. Thus, she became a pioneering "First Lady," since politicians rarely appeared in public with their wives before that. Ching-ling's reign as "First Lady of China" only lasted for two months because that's how long Sun's presidency lasted. I was surprised to learn this, since he is so well known for that role. Much of his fame flows from the Soong family's efforts to mythologize him after he died.

Ching-ling clung to the role of "First Lady of China" for the rest of her life. She sustained her image in the public mind by refusing to be seen with other men. But behind the lofty image, she always felt slighted because the Communist Party would never give her real power. It was too late to rejoin the Nationalists because her younger sister had married their new leader, Chiang Kai-shek. The Party was not big enough for two Grande Dames. To make matters worse, her brother-in-law started killing Communists. Ching-ling took refuge in Moscow and was hailed as a heroine on arrival. But her high-level friends soon informed her that Stalin had executed many of their associates. Now, she was well and truly stuck, and remained that way for the next half century. When Mao Zedong took power, he invited her to join him and gave her a big title; but as a potential rival, he kept her effectively under house arrest. She broke with her family for good when Communist rule began, citing her love of China.

Ching-ling had a fabulous standard of living compared to the unspeakable suffering of her compatriots in the twentieth century. But behind the scenes, she lived with extreme threat. As I read about her, I kept coming across the tortures that Chinese leaders used on their political opponents. These tortures were so disturbing that I had to turn the page or fast-forward the audio. But Ching-ling could not do that. These vivid threats had been part of her reality since childhood, as her father and Sun knew the risks of their political activity. Ching-ling witnessed a lot of violence in China's decades of conflict, and the threat of violence was a constant topic of conversation. As an insider in the Communist coalition, she was aware of their violence too. What could she do?

I pondered this question as I stood in her various living rooms, and I did not have a good answer. We are all swept into the flow of history, and it's easy to feel powerless in the face of events you cannot control. Yet Ching-ling's life was shaped by her own decisions too. She made those decisions with the pathways carved by the extravagant rewards and horrific threats of her unique individual experience.

Chapter Five

Cortisol and Status Stress

Our ancestors lived in a dangerous world, so they built a strong alarm system. We have inherited that system, so we are good at feeling alarmed. When there's no immediate threat, nature's alarm system finds more distant potential threats to warn you about. Threats to your status feel like urgent peril if you're otherwise safe.

Threatened feelings are caused by cortisol, a chemical found in every living thing. Cortisol creates a sense of alarm throughout your whole body because its job is to prepare you for actions that relieve the threat. Cortisol is designed to get your attention. When a gazelle smells a predator, it does not ignore its own alarm system, even though it would rather keep eating. This is why bad feelings are hard to ignore. When your cortisol turns on, you think something is really wrong.

False alarms are part of life. Sometimes a gazelle is panicked by movement in the grass when there's no actual predator. The gazelle soon goes back to enjoying the grass. A gazelle's brain is not big enough to imagine a lion when there is no lion. A human brain is. We can imagine potential future threats in a way that feels real enough to trigger our cortisol. Our babies don't get eaten by lions because we anticipate threats and take preventive action. But you end up with a lot of cortisol when you plug a big human brain into a mammalian operating system.

Your two brains work together to define threat. But your mammal brain cannot tell you in words how it does that, so you only get the verbal brain's side of the story. Your verbal brain notices the bad feeling of cortisol, and looks for evidence of threat. It comes up with a good explanation, and you presume it's true. Each time you do this, you build the pathway that turns on this explanation more easily the next time. But what turned on the cortisol in the first place? We must understand that in order to know why status games feel so threatening.

NATURE'S THREAT DETECTOR

Our brain is designed to learn from pain. We don't have to touch a hot stove twice because our brain learns to recognize the threat the first time. Pain triggers cortisol. Neurons connect when cortisol flows, and that wires us to turn on the cortisol faster in similar future situations. Thus we are wired to anticipate pain and act in time to prevent it. We anticipate pain a lot.

You don't think that with your verbal brain. You just use the pathways you have.

Imagine that a monkey grabs a piece of fruit that a bigger monkey had its eye on. The little monkey gets bitten, and pain triggers cortisol. That paves a pathway between every neuron active at that moment. Thus, without conscious intent, the little monkey learns to anticipate pain when reaching for a resource in the presence of a bigger monkey. It acts to avoid pain by comparing itself to others and restraining its impulse when it perceives relative weakness. It doesn't take many bites to wire this in.

When you were young, whatever triggered your cortisol wired you to anticipate pain from that context in the future. You spend your life trying to avoid everything that caused you pain in the past. But you were not literally bitten by bigger monkeys when you reached for fruit, so it's important to understand what triggered your cortisol.

We humans are born with cortisol. A baby's cortisol surges when its blood sugar is low, because that is nature's signal that you better find food fast. But a baby doesn't know what food is, and has no skills, so it just cries in response to cortisol. Crying is our only inborn skill.

When a newborn elephant is hungry, it walks to its mother's nipple. A gazelle runs to keep up with its mother within hours of its birth. We humans are more helpless and vulnerable at birth than other creatures.

When cortisol triggers a "do something!" feeling, crying is all we can do. But slowly over time, we connect neurons that guide us toward other ways to relieve feeling threatened.

We gradually learn skills to meet our needs, but as fast as we do that, we learn about threats and obstacles to meeting needs. As soon as you learn to walk, you learn that gravity causes pain when you fall. As soon as you learn to call for help, you learn that your calls don't always get answered. You keep experiencing cortisol surges, and learning new ways to relieve the perceived threat.

A baby doesn't understand its true vulnerability, but it still has plenty of cortisol. Over time, it learns to manage that cortisol. It learns to get up when it falls. It learns new ways of asking for help. But the more skill it builds, the more it ventures out into the world of potential threat. Each time we experience pain, we wire ourselves to anticipate pain and thus to protect ourselves.

When you are an adult, you have power you did not have as a child, but you still have old circuits reminding you of your powerlessness. You may be a highly skilled person, and a member of a powerful group, but your mammal brain scans for every possible threat to your power.

DO SOMETHING!

Cortisol works by making you feel bad. No intellectual understanding of threat is needed for cortisol to do its job. The bad feeling simply motivates you to act fast to do whatever makes it stop.

This is easier to understand from the reptile brain's perspective. When a lizard is cold, its brain releases cortisol, and that motivates it to go out into the sun. But it smells predators when it goes out, so it would rather hide under a rock. It only stays out long enough to raise its temperature, and it's on high alert the whole time.

The same is true when a lizard is hungry. It acts to find food and runs back into hiding once the cortisol is relieved. A reptile always faces two bad choices. It survives by weighing the threats and deciding which is more urgent. When you see a lizard sunning itself, you may think it is enjoying inner peace, but it is just running from pain.

A lizard doesn't know what death is. It acts because cortisol feels bad, and relieving cortisol feels good. Reptiles have very little cortex, so they don't do much learning. They rely on skills that are hardwired at birth. Reptiles are so hardwired that they leave home the instant they crack open their shell, and if they don't leave fast enough, a parent eats them. They relieve cortisol with behaviors they inherited from their ancestors.

We humans are not born hardwired with survival skills the way reptiles are. The bigger a creature's cortex, the longer its childhood, because it takes time to wire those neurons with useful survival skills. Humans have a very long childhood compared to other creatures because we have so few skills to start with, and so many neurons available to wire up. But we have a reptile operating system connecting our big cortex to our spine and thus to our body. We must go through our reptile brain to get our body to act. This is why we often feel like we are running from pain. When your reptile brain releases that "do something" chemical, you have a sense of urgency and look for a way to make it stop.

SOCIAL PAIN

Social pain and physical pain go together in the animal world. A baby gazelle gets hungry when it's separated from its mother, and its cortisol surges. That wires the baby to associate pain with separation from its mother.

An isolated gazelle is an easy target for predators, so it seems natural for the brain to associate isolation with pain. But if you had to feel the jaws of a predator before you learned to fear them, few critters would survive. Nature needs a way to wire a young brain to equate social isolation with physical pain without having to get bitten first. It needs a really good way because the stakes are so high.

A triple alarm for social pain is easy to see in a young gazelle. First comes the cortisol of hunger when a young one is separated. Then comes the cortisol of mirror neurons when a young one perceives its mother's agitation after a separation. Finally, the mother typically bites the young one when they reunite. Pain reinforces the circuit that releases a bad feeling when a young gazelle is separated from others.

A young monkey learns to associate social pain with physical pain as well. A monkey is born with enough strength to cling to its mother as she swings through the trees. But it must build the skill of connecting to other monkeys in order to do what it takes to keep its genes alive. This includes skills for getting food, competing for mates, and building alliances for protection from predators.

The stakes rise in puberty, when monkeys and apes leave the group they are born into and migrate to a new troop. Inbreeding is prevented because all males or all females migrate, depending on the species. (Both in a few cases.) Cortisol surges when a young monkey leaves home. If they don't find acceptance elsewhere, their genes will be wiped off the face of the earth. Natural selection built a brain that has life-or-death feelings about social acceptance during puberty.

But acceptance is not enough because a monkey starts at the bottom of the dominance hierarchy of its new troop. It must raise its status in the troop to promote its reproductive success. It is motivated to raise its status because serotonin makes it feel good. When its status-seeking efforts fail, cortisol makes it feel like a survival threat. It can relieve this cortisol by trying again, but the risk of conflict is always there. A monkey is always choosing between the bad feeling of conflict and the bad feeling of giving up.

The same motivational system wires humans to fear isolation, but also to fear domination. Children want to play with others, but when others grab their toys, cortisol is released. The child faces a few bad choices: submission, isolation, or conflict. We don't like to be isolated, but we don't like to be surrounded by people who grab our toys. This dilemma doesn't go away, so each brain navigates it with pathways built from past experience.

Whatever triggered your cortisol when you were young wired you to release cortisol more quickly in similar circumstances. Today's concern with posttraumatic stress can get in the way of making peace with your inner mammal. Every gazelle lives with trauma by today's definition, yet every gazelle functions and meets its needs. A gazelle stays alert for threats, but it also stays focused on rewards. We humans feel threatened by obstacles to the status we desire because old cortisol pathways make the threats feel so real.

When you feel stressed, it's hard to believe that you are causing your stress with pathways built in youth. You put all that behind you, you're convinced, so you see your stress as evidence of the world's flaws. But when you understand the power of your old cortisol pathways, you have power to build new pathways that reduce your cortisol.

Old pathways are hard to accept because they don't make sense to your conscious brain. Those pathways were not built from your conscious decisions; they are just connections among neurons active in a moment of pain. When a horse is whipped by a man with a big hat, the horse fears men with big hats. A hat is a flawed predictor of threat, but the horse doesn't notice. You may have wired in some flawed predictors of threat, but you don't notice if you don't examine your cortisol pathways.

THE GROUP RESPONSE TO STATUS THREATS

When you join a group, you feel a sense of safety for a moment. But now, every threat to your group seems like a survival threat. You have life-and-death feelings about the status of your group without consciously intending to. Rival groups could lower the status of your group, so you see rival groups as survival threats.

A herd animal relies on the group for danger alerts, but also does surveillance for itself. You are always dividing your attention between your group mind and your individual sense. But it's complicated. You could be excommunicated from the group if you don't share its view of the situation, and your mammal brain sees that as a survival threat. So you zoom in on facts that fit your group's perspective, and skim over facts that could be trouble.

SOCIAL DISAPPOINTMENTS TRIGGER CORTISOL

Every time you want something, you risk being disappointed.

It's important to know why disappointment triggers cortisol. Imagine a hungry lion who's just about to catch a gazelle. Suddenly, the gazelle gets away. This is a huge disappointment for the lion because it hasn't eaten in days. It is tempted to keep chasing that gazelle, even as the gap grows bigger and bigger. But if a lion wastes energy on gazelles that got away, it will not have enough energy to catch a better prospect. A successful hunt requires a lion's peak performance, so it would starve to death if it made bad decisions about when to give up.

The brain solves this problem with a huge cortisol surge, which gives the lion a bad feeling about the gazelle it is chasing. The cortisol of disappointment must outweigh the cortisol of hunger in order to end the chase. How a lion knows when that is depends on circuits built from the years it learned to hunt with its mother.

This is why disappointment feels so bad, even when you consciously know that your survival is not threatened.

Let's look at disappointment from the perspective of a chimpanzee watching troop mates enjoy meat from a hunt. The chimp urgently needs meat because protein is scarce in a rainforest diet, and protein provides the strength needed for reproductive success. The chimp doesn't think this consciously, but its dopamine surges when it sees something that meets a need. It tries to grab some of that meat.

We are told that chimpanzees share meat, but this is a gross over-simplification. They share it in the sense that the chimp who caught it hands it over to the strongest chimp, who eats what he wants and then shares it with the next strongest, and so on down the line until there's none left.

So let's say you're a chimp with some confidence in your strength, and you have also built strong ties by grooming the top banana and his allies. You push toward the meat along with other ranking members of your troop. But their huge canine teeth pierce your skin and you feel a surge of pain. They refuse to let you in. What a disappointment!

The stakes are even higher in the mating game. You dare to assert yourself when reproductive opportunity appears, but a stronger rival bares big canine teeth at you. This time, you pull back in time to avoid getting bitten. But you don't give up. You see others succeed, so you continue to look for opportunity and try again. Your strength builds with time, and eventually you succeed. Your genes are immortalized!

Self-assertion is a complex skill. A chimp that never asserted itself would not keep its genes alive, but if they self-asserted recklessly, they would not survive either. Effective assertion is learned from feedback, and disappointment is central to the feedback process. Thus, stress is central to the quest for serotonin.

But cortisol makes you feel like you will die if you don't relieve it fast. When you're disappointed, you urgently look for a way to relieve the feeling. Animals do this with "dogged" persistence, but the big human brain gets philosophical. Maybe you try to avoid disappointment by not wanting anything. Maybe you try to relieve it by blaming others for obstructing your path. Each brain manages disappointment with pathways built from early experience. But each brain has little awareness of its own pathways, so it's easy to take your cortisol as evidence of a real threat.

Children do not have a developed cortex, so they manage these emotions with less philosophy. You see a toy and you want it. If another child takes it, you weigh your options. Every child learns that you can't always get what you want. Playground politics is at the core of the neural networks we bring to adult life. Every child likes to feel important, but every child learns that other kids push back. Every child learns to calibrate their assertions and desires to the anticipated responses of others. Young monkeys spend an enormous amount of time wrestling, and they wire in this skill.

Playground learning is increasingly shaped by adults. Children learn from adults in three major ways: from explicit messages, from the rewards and pain adults actually confer, and by mirroring the way adults seek rewards and avoid pain. Many adults want to protect children from ever having to experience disappointment. This teaches children to protect themselves from disappointment instead of learning to manage it.

Lions fail in 90 percent of their chases. They must manage disappointment to survive.

Monkeys are often disappointed by their grooming partners. After they give a grooming, they fail to get reciprocation, whether a share in meat, protection from enemies, or mating opportunity. The cortisol of disappointment gives them a bad feeling about that grooming partner, so they look for another.

When our expectations of others are disappointed, we release cortisol. It feels like a "betrayal" because your expectations are betrayed. But you don't notice your own expectations, so it feels like the other person truly betrayed you. Cortisol wires you to expect betrayal in those circumstances. You can end up feeling alert for betrayal a lot. You may have learned to blame society for these feelings, so it's useful to remember that animals often betray each other.

A mother chimpanzee lives with the constant risk of kidnapping. This seems hard to believe, but researchers observe stronger females grabbing babies from weaker ones, and refusing to give the child back. The baby dies of dehydration in a few hours, so the risk is extreme. The mother cannot just take the baby back because the kidnapper will hold on until it rips. Thus, a mama chimp is extremely careful about who she allows to approach her. This is hard to do because all female chimps are eager to touch babies and reach out to gratify that desire. It would be nice to trust everyone, but the survival of a mom's genes depend on her vigilance.

When you anticipate recognition from a boss or a romantic prospect, you may not get it. You may feel betrayed. The more you seek recognition, the more you risk feeling betrayed. Cortisol makes it feel like hard evidence of bad will in others.When you understand cortisol, you know how it comes from expectations that you created yourself.

THE ULTIMATE THREAT

Death is the ultimate threat. The big human brain is ominously aware of its own mortality. Your cortex can terrorize your inner mammal with the knowledge that your efforts to survive will eventually fail. You don't know what will kill you, so you stay alert for every possible threat. You don't think this consciously, of course. In fact, we avoid this thought as much as possible with our conscious brain. That makes it hard to recognize the source of the "do something" feeling, and thus find the right relief strategy.

Mortality fears ease when you create something that will survive when you're gone. This meant children for most of human history. Before the age of effective birth control, children came so quickly that you had little time to ponder distant potential threats. Grandchildren came quickly after, and teaching them skills gave you the sense that your unique individual essence would survive.

Today, we have reproductive choices, but few of us get to teach skills to our grandchildren. Thus, we look for other ways to create a legacy and ease our mortality fears. Anything that will survive when you're gone relieves threatened feelings. When a carpenter makes a chair, it feels good to think that the chair will survive. A teacher who helps a student enjoys the sense that the knowledge they have accumulated will survive. People built pyramids, wrote symphonies, and developed technologies because creating something that lasts relieves threatened feelings. Status can enhance your legacy, so it helps relieve cortisol.

But this relief is a two-edged sword, because every threat to your legacy now feels like a survival threat. Every critique of your symphony and every rival technology feels like a survival threat. If your grandchild does not get invited to a party, you feel surprisingly bad, even though you would never consciously think of it as a survival threat. Every threat to your status is magnified because you constantly hear the clock ticking on your legacy.

You can't admit that you have such strong feelings about your own survival, so you focus on a concern for the survival of humanity. But you define the survival of humanity in a way that just happens to promote your legacy. And you still end up with cortisol, because every perceived threat to humanity now feels like a survival threat.

RELIEF AT LAST

Endless cortisol motivates an endless search for relief. Animals relieve cortisol by meeting the specific need that triggered it, whether finding food or escaping a predator. We humans try to do that too, but it's hard because our big cortex is so good at perceiving threats that are not actually present. So we rely on the pathways we have: Whatever brought relief in your past wires you to expect more relief in that way in the future.

For example, if a baboon escapes a lion by climbing up a tree, the great feeling of relief wires it to scan for trees the next time it sees a predator.

If a child escapes conflict in their home by playing video games, the good feeling of relief wires them to think of video games the next time they hear conflict.

If your coworker escapes disturbing thoughts by one-upping you, then will probably try to one-up you again the next time they have disturbing thoughts.

Distraction is popular because it works. It would not work if a real predator lurked, but when threats are imagined you get relief by engaging your mind elsewhere.

Status games are a great distraction. The momentary pleasure of serotonin interrupts unpleasant thoughts so the cortisol stops. Status games can be unpleasant, but they are healthier than many other distractions, such as alcohol, junk food, or aggression. No wonder they're so popular!

As always, this is hard to see in yourself, but so clear in others. A great example is the burial insurance fad a century ago. People were worried about ending up in a pauper's grave for eternity because their family didn't have the funds for a "proper" burial. Many people died young, and many people lived from hand to mouth, so the risk was real. The urge for a high-status burial was so strong that poor people bought burial insurance even if they had to go without food. The insurance man would come each week to collect his ten cents, and you would pay that before you paid the rent. You could die at any moment, and it was comforting to know that your status was secured forever.

Gambling is a classic short-run strategy for feeling like a "winner." Imagine a young person who goes to a casino one day when they're feeling down. They have a big win, and the great surge of reward relieves their distress. They feel like a winner instead of a loser. It wires them to go back to the casino whenever they feel down. They lose all their money, and their status falls. And each time they feel bad, they look to gambling to feel better because that's the only serotonin pathway they've built.

This behavior seems so illogical that it's hard to imagine how a brain can create it. But it's useful to notice what you do when you feel like a "loser." You tell yourself not to think that way, but your verbal brain can't always get relief. So you fall back on some behavior that made you feel like a "winner" long ago. You embrace this behavior with a tenacity that your verbal brain can't quite explain.

The emperors of Ancient Rome lived in constant fear of losing their status due to murderous rivals. They found relief by declaring themselves gods. That was the only way to raise their status since they were already at the peak among humans. But it didn't work for long, since they saw evidence of treachery everywhere—even from the gods.

Imagine seeing a piece of spinach in your teeth after you've just given a presentation. You surge with cortisol when you realize that your spinach was on display all along. The bad feeling wires you to check your teeth next time. But you fear that something else might be wrong, so you keep checking everything you can think of. If you kept monitoring for threats forever, you would not be able to take action toward new rewards. So you learn to shift your focus from threat to rewards. Every mammal does this. A gazelle returns to the pleasure of eating grass as soon as it escapes a predator. In today's world, you can't focus on food all the time, so you reward yourself in other ways. Status seeking has no calories. When you want to relieve a bad feeling, your mind drifts toward anything that raised your status in the past.

Status games may be stressful, but they relieve the stress of more painful thoughts, and that gets us hooked. Each brain seeks relief with pathways built from its own experience. Whatever relieved stress for you in the past is now your urgent desire because you don't know how to stop threatened feelings without it. When you see this urgency in others, you may think it looks foolish. But when you chase your own self-soothing tool, it seems like a necessity.

Your quality of life depends on your ability to manage your cortisol. We are born into cortisol, but we gradually learn to manage it without consciously trying to. A baby stops crying when it hears its mother's footsteps. Over time, a child cries less because it learns better ways to meet its needs. But its awareness of threat also increases with time, so its growing skills do not prevent cortisol.

When you are born, you are at the top of the status hierarchy in the sense that your needs are met by others. You just scream and people rush to serve you. But all too soon, you realize that your cries do not control the world, and crying can even make things worse. So as you grow in power, you become aware of the limits to your power even faster. This dilemma is at the core of every one of us. Every brain struggles to feel safe despite the powerlessness of its early experience.

THE STATUS GAMES OF ALEXANDER HAMILTON

Hamilton's "country" home in the north of Manhattan is easy to visit. I went there to ponder his choice to die for status.

Hamilton had good judgment about many things, so his bad judgment about dueling is a mystery. At first, I thought he wanted to die to atone for betraying his family. But as I dug deeper, I discovered his enormous early experience with "honor" and with death. Dying for honor would seem reasonable from his perspective.

In his adolescence, he wrote to a friend: "I would willingly risk my life, though not my character, to exalt my station." The exact same sentiment is expressed by Sigmund Freud in an early letter: "I could gladly throw away my life for one great moment." Such thoughts are eerily similar to young male monkeys risking their lives to gain mating opportunity. Young male humans have always taken risks to gain the status necessary to win a desirable bride and support offspring. Hamilton and Freud put it in writing.

But Hamilton's early experience left him with a greater incentive to risk everything for status. He was a "bastard" at a time when that meant exclusion from most institutions—even school! His social status was a jumble because his parents had an upper-class background but lived in poverty.

Hamilton's career began at age eleven, when he was orphaned. He got a full-time job and was so effective that he was left in charge of the business by age fourteen. He was then adopted into a well-to-do family, and he read the books they admired in his spare moments at work. He grew into a powerful mix of upper-class manners and lower-class ambition.

Hamilton survived epidemics, insurrections, and floods in his early years, so he would have positive expectations about his ability to survive. He took big risks and got big rewards.

But big rewards did not make him happy because he always felt like an outsider. When he went to America for college, he felt like an outsider because he did not belong to one of the thirteen colonies like his compatriots. He was the first "American" in the sense that he identified with the United States rather than an individual state. He rose to the top of the new country, but continued to feel one-down.

He had good reason to feel threatened, because he was harshly attacked in public discourse. He didn't need to take it personally, since top-ranking mammals are always attacked by rivals for those top spots. But when you're the one being attacked, it's hard not to take it personally.

What surprised me was that they attacked him for being a "monarchist." After all he'd done to establish the US Constitution, why would they say that? As I researched this puzzle, I learned a lot about my fellow mammals.

First, I discovered the nastiness of partisan politics at that time. The Founding Fathers cooperated as long as they had a common enemy. Once they beat the British, they fought each other for status. The higher a person's status, the more rivals would be coveting their position. But your rivals cannot acknowledge their own lust for status. They come up with greater-good arguments to justify their assertions. They need arguments that people will accept. Since people feared monarchy in those days, accusing Hamilton of monarchism worked.

Second, Hamilton had the kind of accent associated with European aristocrats. The Caribbean manner of expression he'd grown up with had the courtly tone of upper-class Europe. He sounded like the enemy. Paradoxically, he was criticized for sounding lower class too, because he was more assertive than a "gentleman" was supposed to be. He was condemned for having "ambition." Hamilton was like a gazelle whose stripes don't match any familiar pattern.

Third, the two parties polarized around different views of current events. Hamilton saw the French Revolution through the lens of the violent insurrections he lived through in the Caribbean. Thomas Jefferson saw the French Revolution through the lens of his five fabulous years as ambassador to France. He'd been busy shopping for wine and philosophizing with painted women, so the guillotine and the Terror barely pierced his thoughts about France. The conflicting views on policy toward France led to the two-party system in the United States today. Each party used sophisticated legal language to make the other party's position sound like a survival threat. Once one view is neurochemically wired in, a mammal rarely sees alternatives.

When Hamilton was challenged to a duel, his response was not unusual for his time. And since he'd always been defensive about his honor, he might be extra susceptible. The spot where he was killed is open to visitors, but I decided to skip it. Such a sad experience is not worth the drive to New Jersey. Instead, I walked past his former home on Wall Street, trying to imagine it as a small-town scene. When New York's population was tiny, it throbbed with the same status games as any cosmopolis today because we're all mammals.

Chapter Six

Why It's Always
High School in Your Brain

Neuroplasticity peaks in adolescence, so the pathways we build in those years get quite large. No one intends to see the world through a lens built in high school, but big neural pathways are so efficient that we rely on them for life without conscious intent. The power of old neural pathways rests on a substance called *myelin*. It coats neurons the way insulation coats wire, making them super-fast conductors of electricity. Your myelinated neurons conduct your brain's electricity so easily that you rely on them a lot. Myelin dips after adolescence, so our myelinated pathways are built from our experiences in adolescence and earlier.

Myelin peaks at age two. Then it plateaus, and actually dips by age eight. In puberty, it spurts again, so your teen experiences build the final refinements of your neural network. You can learn after that, of course, but without myelin, it's different. The electricity in your brain has a hard time flowing down an unmyelinated pathway. Myelinated neurons conduct electricity up to a hundred times faster. The zip of electricity along a myelinated pathway gives us the feeling that we know what is going on. So we often choose to flow into old pathways, even when they don't exactly fit the facts. We're not aware of this choice, but we can become aware of it if we understand it.

The world constantly floods you with more detail than you could possibly process. If you tried to process every sensory input, you would not make sense of anything. So you are making choices all the time about which sensory inputs to focus on and whether to interpret them as new occurrences of old patterns. For example, when you see an animal in the distance on a hike, you quickly decide whether it fits your stored image of a cute pet or something dangerous.

You were not born knowing what a dog is. Each child builds the concept from repeated experience. A two-year-old learns to distinguish a dog from a cat. And it can look at a dog from the back and still determine that it fits the "dog" pattern. It even learns to differentiate animals that it has only seen in storybooks. The myelin of youth builds big pathways from whatever inputs the child receives repeatedly.

You use those pathways for the rest of your life because your electricity flows into them so easily. The electricity in your brain flows like water in a storm, finding the paths of least resistance. If you see something that does not fit a pattern you've already stored, you have no meaning to attach to it. What can you do?

You can construct a new meaning by connecting bits and parts of old circuits. But this takes so much focus that you have to stop whatever else you're doing. So you make a decision. If the new input is not urgently important, you just let it flow into the best match you have. You might even ignore it, without consciously intending to, because the electricity in your brain has trouble jumping across the synapses between unmyelinated neurons. If the flow is not super-charged by a sense of urgency, the message will peter out. This is why old pathways shape our awareness without our knowing it.

You don't have to remember the experiences that built your pathways in order for them to shape your thinking. You are not thinking about the old experience when you use the old pathway. You literally just go with the flow.

Your big pathways built up from repetition, emotion, and myelin. Emotion means the happy and unhappy chemicals that mark an input as good for you or bad for you. One child may have negative associations for a dog, and another has positive associations, depending on the chemicals released in their own experience. Emotions are the brain's way of tagging information as important—as a way to meet needs or a threat to be avoided. Emotions strengthen neural pathways to help you get rewards or avoid harm in the future.

So whatever you experienced repeatedly and emotionally in your myelin years built the superhighways of your brain. You rely on these pathways without noticing because they work so well. This is why we tend to see our adult experiences as new chapters of our old story.

You can learn to notice this if you invest some effort. You can find the patterns in your early experience and see how you are relying on them today. This works in the opposite direction too—find the patterns in your present and see how they fit your early experience. With practice, you will see how you rely on an old lens to interpret your present. Your old lens is just a random collection of experiences rather than Absolute Truth. Knowing this frees you from jumping to the same conclusions again and again. It frees you to find new ways to interpret your experiences.

Each brain has a unique collection of neural pathways, but our brains are similar because our experiences are similar. We all start life weak and dependent. We all feel the pain of gravity when we fall. We all have new urges in adolescence. Most important, we all have chemicals that create life-or-death feelings about meeting our needs.

Children build mental models of the social world in the same way that they learn about the physical world. In adolescence, you have new experiences and thus add to your mental model of the world. But our core operating system is the same: We strive to repeat behaviors that feel good and avoid behaviors that feel bad. In the state of nature, this works, because things that feel good are good for the survival of your genes. In the modern human world, we use our big brains to think about long-run good, but we also want to feel good in the short run. This is the conundrum that we all have to manage. In adolescence, you face it with a limited stock of experience. Your good and bad feelings are strong, and they wire you to expect more good and bad feelings in similar ways. This is the challenge of being human.

Animals often transfer to new groups at puberty, and the myelin of puberty helps. New groups require new learning about the physical and social environment. Our ancestors often joined new groups to get mates. They often had to learn a new language, new customs, and a new way to get home in the dark. The myelin of puberty evolved to help a mammal store new information about meeting its future survival needs. So even if you think you've left your teen experiences behind, they shape your emotions a lot.

POPULARITY

Your verbal brain may ridicule the concept of "popularity," but your mammal brain relies on pathways built by past emotion. The facts about popularity can help you understand your brain. Popularity is a real thing in the sense that sociologists get consistent answers when they ask students to rank popularity in a school. Students even report their own popularity with surprising accuracy. This is remarkable since the hierarchy is informal rather than explicit. Each brain simply observes its fellow mammals and arrives at the same conclusions. Your mirror neurons alert you when others get rewards or pain, and you learn to expect rewards and pain in similar ways. Just like monkeys.

High-school popularity rests on the same characteristics that determine reproductive success in monkeys: a healthy appearance, strong social alliances, and a tolerance for risk. High school students are not consciously trying to spread their genes, but monkeys are not consciously doing it either. We mammals just try to do what feels good, and natural selection built a brain that rewards you with good feelings when you do things that spread your genes. Behaviors that stimulate serotonin promote reproductive success, so teens look for ways to stimulate serotonin. This is why adolescents are so motivated to improve their appearance, build social bonds, and take risks.

We define these traits in different ways, depending on our lived experience.

Healthy appearance is defined in different ways, as each mammal observes the traits associated with social dominance. Biologists have found that traits attractive to mates are always valid indicators of fitness. The famous peacock's tail is a reliable indicator of a strong immune system. The traits that attract mates in high school may not seem like reliable fitness indicators, but nose piercings can be thought of as a display of willingness to take risks and to invest in a social alliance. Humans have used a wide range of adornments to attract mates because we're so motivated to imitate a trait that seems to get rewarded. When a tight corset got rewards, corsets got tighter and tighter.

Social alliances make a mammal attractive because they convey strength. Teen social alliances come in many forms: street gangs, study groups, social media, athletic teams, formal positions in student organizations, and the iconic table in the cafeteria. When we see people in social alliances get rewards, it motivates us to build social alliances. With intense competition for good mates, you seek the strongest alliance you can find.

Risk tolerance can be displayed in many ways: adventure sports, academic challenges, crime, and the all-important face-to-face chat with an attractive potential mate. Teens take huge risks with no obvious reward if they see risk takers rise in popularity. In the animal world, huge risks are often necessary for reproductive success. We have inherited a brain selected for risk tolerance. Each brain weighs risks with pathways built from its own past experience.

The popularity problem has no neat solution. The harsh truth is that some monkeys get more attention than others. Primatologists have found that wild monkeys spend a lot of time gazing at the alpha of their group. We have inherited a brain that monitors high-status group mates in order to meet its needs.

When young humans gather, their attention converges on high-status individuals. Imagine a high school cafeteria with a table full of "popular" kids. You watch them laughing and enjoying themselves without consciously intending to. You may feel left out and even hate them for excluding you. But the number of seats at that table is limited, and people have a right to choose their lunch mates. The popular kids did not cause your bad feeling. You caused it yourself with your own one-down thoughts. It's easy to blame your feelings on them because you're not aware of your mammalian social-comparison impulse. Your one-down feelings make it easy to bond with students who feel left out too. One-down feelings get rewards, of a sort, because social groups form easily around shared resentments. Thus, people keep triggering the bad feeling of exclusion in order to enjoy the good feeling of inclusion.

Adolescent angst is widely blamed on social media today. Social platforms provide a convenient way to project a healthy appearance, build a social alliance, and take risks. Popularity is hard to build in real life, so short cuts are highly desired. Each generation expresses primal impulses with the tools available. Respect and recognition are hard to get, so each generation rushes toward any new opportunities that appear. We hope to beat the competition, but we soon see our fellow status-seeking mammals overrun the opportunities we set our sights on.

Celebrities often say that they were not popular in high school, and our personal acquaintances often say the same. How is it possible that no one was ever popular?

One explanation is that popular people are a tiny percentage, and you don't cross paths with them.

Another explanation is that no one feels popular because we never live up to our idealized expectation of endless one-up feelings.

A third explanation is that people claim they were not popular because it's today's way to be popular. Outsider status is rewarded today, so everyone rushes to display outsider status.

A final explanation is that we are embarrassed by our adolescent yearnings for popularity, so we deny their existence. We know better with our adult brains, so we disdain our adolescent quest for popularity. We deny impulses that we don't think in words, though we still have the pathways that turn on our chemicals.

All of these explanations are true, which is why the adolescent urge for popularity can be so pervasive and yet so ignored.

TEEN STATUS VS. ADULT STATUS

When a popular classmate is a washout in adulthood, you enjoy the news. You one-up them at last! You don't admit this consciously, of course. The German language has a word for taking pleasure in the suffering of others: s*chadenfreude*. When others lose status, your high-school brain sees it as a gain in your status.

The fallen high-school hero is a common pattern because traits that make you popular in high school do not necessarily get rewarded in adulthood. This is why parents strive to steer their children toward skills with long-run value. But parents often fail because peer approval has more reward power in a brain that evolved to reproduce.

It's hard for adolescents to choose future rewards over present rewards, so adults did not give their offspring a choice for most of human history. Teens were sent to apprenticeships with other families instead of being left to pursue immediate rewards. Apprentices were often treated harshly, so young people learned to manage their impulses to avoid pain. Self-restraint helps you succeed in the future, even if it doesn't make you popular in a herd of adolescents.

In the 1960s, old customs were uprooted. Parents were told to honor their children's impulses. Children were effectively given the one-up position. We were told this is natural, but it is not. Young apes must impress their elders before they get mating opportunity. Tribal humans had to impress their elders to get mating opportunity as well. In the past, young people did not expect the one-up position to be handed to them. They learned to work for good feelings instead of seeing them as a right. Children learned the real consequences to their actions. They learned that butter is only available if the cow is nurtured and the milk is churned. Children had to help out to enjoy such luxuries.

To understand today's mindset, it's important to know that high school is a relatively recent phenomenon. In the past, few people got a secondary education, and if they did, it was not in a large institution. Adolescents spent more time in mixed-age company. In a modern high school, teens outnumber adults. This makes it tempting for teens to mirror the behavior of other teens, and court teen approval rather than adult approval.

The brain learns from pain as well as rewards, and in the past, poor choices led to pain. You could flunk a course, and even flunk out of school. Today, social promotion means you're rewarded whether or not you meet fixed criteria. College is available whether or not you study in high school, or work and save to pay for it. Young people can easily wire themselves to see peer status as the most important thing in life.

This pattern is reinforced by adults with the anti-authority mindset. Opposition to societal norms is applauded by many parents and teachers. Adolescents quickly learn that they can get rewards by being oppositional instead of by learning essential self-management skills.

Students who make healthy long-run choices risk being "unpopular" during their adolescent neuroplasticity. They can wire in a one-down feeling even if they don't consciously agree with it. And students who neglect their studies and chase popularity end up with one-down feelings in a different way. They may fail to build essential mind-management skills when they focus on peer approval, and feel one-down when others' skills seem greater. Each brain sees its own weaknesses because that helped our ancestors survive.

This dilemma has no simple solution. One-down feelings are part of life. Our quality of life depends on our ability to manage these feelings. Teens have less experience with managing them, so they often rely on a strategy known as "cool."

THE QUEST TO BE "COOL"

"Cool" has many meanings but they all revolve around hiding distress and weakness. A toddler shows distress when a favorite toy is grabbed, but adolescents learn to hide their distress and appear strong. They strive to look "cool," even when they feel one-down.

When "cool" gets rewards, you wire yourself to do it again. If you impress your peers by suppressing your fear, the good feeling of approval wires you to suppress your fear again. You could do this by filling your verbal brain with one-up thoughts, so you feel superior to those who seem threatening. You could also do it by saying you don't care about whatever is distressing you. You are too cool to care. Whatever works wires you to do it again.

However you define cool, it seems urgently important to your mammal brain. Like a baboon who escapes a lion by climbing a tree, the great feeling of relief wires you to scan for a cool pose the next time you feel threatened. Familiar examples are partying, being oppositional, developing an admired skill, and simply cutting yourself off from your feelings. Let's see how these thought habits create one-up feelings and relieve one-down feelings.

Partying is cool because it distracts you from the source of your distress. It relieves cortisol by shifting your thoughts away from potential threats. If you get attention and respect at the party, one-up feelings replace one-down feelings. This trains your mammal brain to think partying solves your problems, even when you do nothing about the real problem. The next time you feel distressed, you expect partying to replace the bad feeling with a good feeling because the pathway is there. The problem might get worse, and the newness of partying wears off, so you might have to escalate the partying to keep getting relief.

Being oppositional means rejecting anything that makes you feel weak. You can say you hate school, you hate your family, you hate society, you hate the sexy classmate who doesn't return your affection. Whether you act on this hatred or just dwell on it in your mind, the pathway builds. You enjoy a one-up feeling when you oppose things that distress you. The animal perspective helps us see why. Animals rarely attack predators because they know they would lose. But in exceptional cases, such as a mother protecting her child or a group that can win with joint action, the brain releases testosterone and the animal attacks instead of running. Such attacks are tremendously risky in the real world, but teens live in a protective bubble. They may attack without regard to the risk and enjoy the cool sense of strength.

Focusing on a skill is another way to be cool. It could be athletic skill, academic skill, or artistic talent. Your brain notices which skills get recognition in your world, and you expect the good feeling of recognition when you build the skill. Whenever you feel one-down, you can engage in the skill and feel one-up. When you feel weak, your special skill helps you feel strong. It relieves bad thoughts so quickly that you don't know you're using it for that purpose. You don't recognize the distress that motivates you or develop other modes of managing that distress.

Cutting yourself off from your feelings is a strategy that a big human brain is capable of. An animal would not survive if it ignored its feelings. It would not know when to find food or run from predators. Animals have false alarms sometimes, and run when it's not necessary. Humans have false alarms a lot because we're so good at generalizing. We feel foolish if we run when there's no predator, so we try to ignore our internal alarms. You might even win the admiration of your peers when you ignore your internal alarm, since they are struggling to manage their own threatened feelings. But in the long run, ignoring your feelings is like driving with your foot on the brake. You suffer a lot of wear and tear, and you don't see your own power to relieve it because you've stopped noticing that your foot is on the brake.

Cool strategies get myelinated with repetition. In adulthood, those pathways are so efficient that you don't notice them—you think you are just seeing the world as it is. Of course, you don't consciously embrace your teen thought loops. You add a veneer of adult sophistication. You find a "good reason" to justify your cool behavior. But your habitual response is hard to stop because your cortisol surges when you think of doing something "uncool." Here are some examples.

Imagine it's Saturday night, and you are exhausted. You long to just go to bed, but it's "uncool" to go to bed early on a Saturday night. You don't want to feel like a "loser," so you force yourself to go out, without really knowing why. The point is not that your pajamas are the best option. The point is that you are weighing the options with an old pathway without realizing it.

Imagine that you hate a person who is doing better than you. They haven't harmed you, but your intense hostility won't go away. You might notice a strong similarity between this person and those who one-upped you in youth. You feel one-down until you think badly of this person, and then you feel better. You don't know why you do this because we're not aware of our pathways.

Imagine that you break your wrist and can't practice a skill that you've enjoyed since high school. A doomsday feeling suddenly overtakes you. You can't explain the feeling since the injury does not affect your satisfying job and loving family. The feeling would make sense if you could rewind the tape of your life. You would see that you relieved distress with this skill in the past. Now your reliable way to feel good is gone. You don't know how to be cool without it.

Distress comes to everyone because we all seek a position of strength and feel disappointed when we fail when we succeed, we fear losing the position of strength that we've gained. Reliable ways to feel strong are prized because they give you reliable relief from feelings of weakness. One teen might get a strong feeling from shoplifting while another gets it from chess tournaments. One might get power from being cooperative while another gets it from being uncooperative. Repetition builds a highway that turns on faster in the future.

You might get frustrated when you notice the power of high-school brain. You might blame "our society," and imagine a perfect world where every young person gets wired for perfect happiness. To see how unrealistic this is, let us return to the natural predicament of adolescence.

KING OF THE WORLD

Every young person wants to be "special" because the serotonin feels good. Every brain longs for center stage, but must live in a world in which seven billion others long for center stage. We spend our youth adapting to this harsh fact of life. In adolescence, we gain a new tool for doing that: daydreaming. Animals and children don't daydream because a big cortex is necessary. A teen brain can suddenly imagine itself as top dog in a way that feels real enough to stimulate happy chemicals. You can always be king of the world in your own mind.

Big dreams can motivate action. Our ancestors blazed new trails because they imagined big rewards. Big dreams are the motivational strategy of today's education system. In the past, students were motivated with carrots and sticks, but that has become taboo. Today, students are encouraged to imagine themselves being "big."

Imagining your future importance feels good. But this motivational strategy has problems. Sometimes, it substitutes for action instead of motivating action. Teens can enjoy the feeling of future importance without taking steps to make it happen. Disappointment triggers cortisol.

And even when students do take action, their reality always seems to fall short of their superstar dreams. More cortisol.

Dreams of grandeur are like drugs—they feel good in the short run but hurt you in the long run. Like a drug addict, you habituate to the high you already have, so it takes bigger and bigger dreams to keep feeling it. When reality disappoints, you rush to your big dream to feel better. Repetition wires you to see yourself as king of the world. You're wired to zoom in on information that fits this worldview, and ignore information that conflicts with your expectations. This leaves you far from the realism that girds a person for success in adulthood. But it's hard to let go of the grandiose mindset when your teachers, friends, and sometimes even family reinforce it. A person may actively exclude inputs that offend their royal self-image, and lose touch with reality.

Dreams have value, but they are not enough. If a young person fails to make progress in real life, they need more than dreaming. They need to take effective action steps, and they need adults who withhold rewards unless the person takes effective action steps. If you reward young people when they don't take effective action, you wire them to expect rewards without taking effective action.

One grandiose dream is so pervasive that it's hard to transcend: the dream of becoming a hero by rescuing others. Adolescents have always dreamed of saving their community, and that has morphed into "saving the world." To a young brain, it feels great to imagine yourself as a world-saving hero. You get respect from peers and adults when you profess this ambition. You might not get respect if you profess more self-centered plans. You might even be condemned as "selfish" if you focus on just supporting yourself. You see the respect that others get when embrace the rescue mindset, and you want that. You feel one-up as soon as you declare your intent to rescue others, whether or not you actually make anything better. The feeling is so rewarding that it distracts you from more realistic paths to rewards.

OPPRESSED AND DOWNHEARTED

What happens when life disappoints your big dreams?

Cortisol surges. You look for a way to explain this bad feeling. You see people who have what you want. You conclude that they are the source of your problem.

Cortisol creates a "do something!" feeling. You look for something to do to relieve it. Fighting those who have what you want seems like the solution. If you don't have the strength to take down a rival yourself, you look for social alliances to get that strength. Humans often spend their lives building alliances to fight perceived oppressors in order to feel good. They don't end up feeling good, alas, because their mammal brain keeps striving for more one-up positions. Life always disappoints the dream of endless effortless serotonin.

A healthier way to live is to know why serotonin dips so that the dips feel less threatening. But the dips you experienced in adolescence wired you to fear those particular dips in the future. The status frustrations you lived with during puberty built cortisol pathways that make it easy to feel the same status frustrations today.

One-down feelings are part of life, but adolescents have more of them for an important reason: They start comparing themselves to adults instead of children. They start coveting adult rewards instead of lollipops. The result is a keen sense of their relative weakness.

This bad feeling is heightened when a teenager sees another teen get adult rewards. When another teen earns money or gets public recognition or the all-important "reproductive opportunity," one-down feelings surge. Neurons connect when cortisol flows, making it easier to feel bad each time you hear about someone else getting a desirable reward. Cortisol is so good at doing its job that you're sure something awful is happening. You look around for bad stuff to explain the feeling. Lots of bad news is on offer from people trying to recruit you into their alliance. You can end up with a very negative perspective.

Humans have always struggled to overcome their negative bias. Cultures have struggled to teach young people to transcend envy. But today's educational philosophy is different. It teaches young people that social injustice has deprived them of the master-of-the-universe position to which they are entitled. This enticing message can boost a teacher's popularity. Repetition builds the pathway, and it starts to feel obviously true. Status games get deeply rooted into people who insist that they don't care about status.

THE STATUS GAMES OF EDWARD DE VERE, EARL OF OXFORD, AKA SHAKESPEARE

I visited Shakespeare's Birthplace in Stratford-on-Avon, and was thrilled to be surrounded by five-hundred-year-old buildings. It got me thinking about Shakespeare as a flesh-and-blood person, so I looked for more information. That's how I discovered the evidence that "Shakespeare" was a pen name for Edward de Vere, 17th Earl of Oxford. The suggestion seemed paranoid to me at first, but the more I learned, the more obvious it seemed. Scholars still debate the identity of Shakespeare, and the majority still believe that Shakespeare was, in fact, the merchant William Shakspere of Avon. Whether or not you see De Vere as the author of the Shakespeare plays, his life story is amazing. His status bounced from top to bottom as Elizabethan status games swirled around him.

Edward de Vere was heir to the highest peerage in England. His father presided over the coronation of Queen Elizabeth, and half a century later, Edward would officiate at her funeral and the coronation of her successor. Status didn't bring him happiness, alas. In the 1500s, minor acts of nonconformity could bring treason charges that got your head cut off. The Earl of Oxford knew people who had ended up on the chopping block, so the threat felt quite real. Yet he had a natural mammalian urge to be special.

When Edward was eleven years old, his parents hosted a visit from Queen Elizabeth. He was sent home from his tutor at Cambridge University to join the festivities. In those days, it was common for nobles to entertain their monarch, and plays were often performed for the occasion. Edward's father had his own theatrical troop for this purpose, and young Edward was there to experience it.

Shortly after the event, Dad died under mysterious circumstances. That made young Edward the legal ward of Queen Elizabeth. She had him brought to London in a procession of 120 white horses, and fostered him in the home of her chief minister, William Cecil. The top scholars in England were brought in to tutor him in a different subject every hour of the day. In Cecil's home, Edward lived with the second largest library in England. At age fourteen, Edward was sent to Oxford University, where he learned what was then known about astronomy, anatomy, mathematics, and history. He spoke many languages and had advanced skill in many arts and athletics. His graduation was attended by Elizabeth, and then he went to law school at the Inns of Court. De Vere may have been the most educated person in history.

But what he liked was theater. Early experience had shown him the power of theater to please and also to persuade. The young Earl wanted to study theater in Italy, where a hot new form of social media called commedia dell'arte had caught on. Any parent might object to this plan, and de Vere's foster father was a Puritan who saw theater as the devil's playground. Cecil had other plans for the young aristocrat: to marry him to Cecil's own daughter. This would make Cecil's future grandson an Earl, a huge reward for this man who presided over nobles but was not one himself.

Fortunately for de Vere, the Queen loved plays. She consented to his plan, and he spent over a year in Europe in exactly the places where the Shakespeare plays are set. When he returned to London, he started writing plays that were performed in court.

A royal court is hard to understand from today's perspective. Imagine every high-status person in the country hanging around a castle day and night with no clear job description. There was nothing to do but to vie for recognition from the Queen. De Vere got recognition because his plays made people laugh.

But it was complicated because his plays were like *Saturday Night Live*. They poked fun at courtiers in ways that insiders understood. People began to resent the young Earl who was the center of attention. He made it worse by wearing strange clothes that he'd brought back from Italy. But de Vere kept producing plays for courtiers, and even sponsored drama troops like his father did. He soon ran low on funds, alas, because his status as the Queen's ward gave her rights to his inheritance, and Cecil implemented those rights with brutal efficiency.

More trouble bubbled when de Vere's drama friends leaked scripts of his plays to printers. Printing was the hot new technology of the time—a low-cost way to reach a huge audience compared to handwritten manuscripts. Printing was highly censored in those days, but readers were so eager for good material that printers took chances. Works were often published without an author's name, and the first Shakespeare plays appeared with no name on them. But Cecil worried about embarrassing the government, and looked for a way to stop Lord Oxford's hobby.

This is when the history plays of "Shakespeare" began to appear, and also when the Queen began paying de Vere a thousand pounds a year for life, through an executive order that specifically forbade accounting for services rendered. These history plays were great PR for the English monarchy, and they glorified de Vere's ancestors as well as Elizabeth's. It seems that the Queen didn't want the public to know that the plays came from the court, for that would make them seem like propaganda. The project was a huge success in creating a sense of nationhood for the English. They were a bunch of warring dukedoms before the Tudors, and the "Shakespeare" histories played a huge role in building a national identity.

You may find it hard to believe that a writer of such merit would give up credit for his work. But remember that Lord Oxford already had top status, and any resistance could bring treason charges that got him executed or worse. (If you wonder what's worse than being executed, research torture in that period.) The risk of decapitation was impossible to forget because the severed heads of traitors were perched on city gates for everyone to see.

And there was a bigger problem. The Queen refused to marry, and without an heir, England could revert to civil war. Her distrust of marriage is easy to understand because she grew up knowing that her father had chopped off her mother's head. Elizabeth was close to the ax herself when her Catholic older sister was on the throne. As Elizabeth's fertile years neared their end, anxiety about succession was frantic. What could be done?

William Cecil was a take-charge guy who had solved the Queen's problems for years. One theory is that he helped arrange a secret marriage between the Queen and de Vere before the young man's trip to Italy. That would produce a legitimate blue-blood heir without Elizabeth having to yield to a husband in public. The child would be passed off as the son of an aristocrat and then acknowledged when the time was right.

But when the time was right, the child was an unruly teen who refused to play ball. The child is allegedly the Earl of Southampton, the person to whom the first works of "Shakespeare" are dedicated. The name "Shakespeare" appeared for the first time on the long poem "Venus and Adonis," about a powerful older woman seducing a younger man. (You can't make this stuff up!) Page one of the published book is a dedication to Southampton, who was twenty years old by then. The lad is also believed to be the "fair youth" of the sonnets.

Scholars have always struggled to explain the young man's relationship to "Shakespeare." Southampton's back story is eerily familiar. His father died in mysterious circumstances when he was nine years old, and he became a ward of court living in Cecil's home. When he came of age, Cecil insisted that the boy marry Cecil's granddaughter—the child of de Vere's marriage to Cecil's daughter. That would have put de Vere's genes on the throne as well as Cecil's, but young Southampton refused to marry the girl. He may have thought of himself as king of the hill rather than Cecil's pawn. Cecil may have withdrawn his support for the young man. De Vere risked treason charges if he opined on the matter, and his poem seems to be a safer way to hint at the existence of an heir. These works were huge best-sellers at the time, though most copies have mysteriously disappeared.

Cecil was quite old by this time, but before he died, he managed to install his son Robert as the Queen's right-hand man. Robert cut a secret deal with a different successor while the Queen slowly expired. Southampton got tired of waiting around, so he planned an uprising with another young Earl. The night before the uprising, the plotters staged a public performance of Shakespeare's *Richard III*—a special performance with an added scene showing Richard handing the crown to his challenger. Richard was presented as a Robert-Cecil look-alike. The real-life uprising failed, however, and the conspirators were locked up in the Tower.

They were condemned to death by a jury of "peers" that included de Vere. He was forced to rubber-stamp the treason verdict against his own alleged son. But it seems like he cut a deal behind the scenes. The facts are public record: When the other plotters were decapitated, Southampton remained in the Tower. When Elizabeth died, the first act of the new king was to free Southampton from the Tower. James freed him by messenger before he even left Scotland for London, and Southampton's confiscated property was restored too. It seems like de Vere saved Southampton's life by relinquishing all claims to the throne and supporting Cecil's pawn, James I. And it seems like the deal gagged the name "Shakespeare" for many years because it had become associated with hints of a true heir.

No new "Shakespeare" works appeared in print for twenty years. The complete works of "Shakespeare" were finally published thirty years later by de Vere's son-in-law. The First Folio included eighteen plays that had never been seen before. Where were the manuscripts? None has ever been found. The First Folio hinted that "Shakespeare" was from Avon, though there were many Avons at the time, and the Stratford merchant now credited as the author never claimed to be a playwright while he was alive. De Vere's son-in-law seems to have found a way to keep the work alive while also keeping himself alive.

Then this drama went dark because the Puritans took over and shut down all the theaters. When the Restoration opened them decades later, the plays were suddenly popular, but their author was unknown except for the word "Shakespeare." Anyone who could have known more was dead.

Imagine de Vere's grief at the end of his life. Instead of enjoying the immortality of his creations, he was anonymous except to his office staff. This pain is expressed in Hamlet's dying words, "What a wounded name shall live behind me, things standing thus unknown." Hamlet said these words to Horatio, and de Vere actually had a young cousin Horatio. It's easy to imagine the dying author begging his cousin, in Hamlet's words, "In this harsh world, draw thy breath in pain to tell my story."

I felt tremendous kinship for someone who kept writing throughout these tribulations. I wanted to visit his home and stand where he stood. Unfortunately, London burned in 1666, and the relevant places are gone. De Vere's letters to William Cecil from college and from Italy survive in the archives of Robert Cecil's country home. I was eager to go there and touch the paper he touched. Alas, you have to be an accredited researcher to be admitted, and I did not meet the criteria. I will visit the remains of the de Vere family castle in rural Essex as soon as I can travel. Until then, I was thrilled to learn that Southampton's childhood home was turned into a hotel that I have already stayed in!

Part 3

HEALTHY ALTERNATIVES TO STATUS GAMES

Chapter Seven

A Healthy Serotonin Mindset

The natural urge for serotonin confronts us with a difficult trade-off: to seek social recognition or not to seek it. Seeking can lead to conflict and disappointment, but not seeking can lead to resentment and despair. What's a modern mammal to do?

We can carve a middle path between the extreme of endless striving and the extreme of giving up.

And we can learn to value this middle path for its effective trade-off between cortisol and serotonin.

The middle path is hard to maintain, however, because the extremes are so alluring. To enjoy the middle lane, you must consciously choose it over and over. Imagine yourself driving on the middle lane of a highway. You get stuck behind a slow car, so you pull into the fast lane. Once you're there, you just keep up instead of going back. The next day, you start out in the middle lane, but another car tails close behind, so you pull into the slow lane. Then, it seems hard to get back into the middle lane, so you just stay in the slow lane. If you don't make a conscious effort to stay in the middle lane, it will be out of reach.

LIFE IN THE MIDDLE LANE

It's hard to notice the middle lane, and that makes it hard to choose. You notice the fast lane because it has a glamorous identity. You notice the slow lane because it has an easy-going vibe. The middle lane doesn't seem cool in any way. No one prides themselves on being a "middle-lane person."

If you go with the flow, you are likely to end up in the slow lane watching others whiz by, or in the fast lane with endless cortisol. Sticking to the middle lane is a learned skill. It doesn't mean you're there all the time. You can grasp opportunities in the fast lane and protection in the slow lane when it makes sense, but you steer yourself back to the middle lane afterward. You can build the skill of returning to the middle lane. It starts with understanding your brain's attraction to the fast lane and the slow lane.

THE LURE OF THE FAST LANE

The joy of the fast lane is obvious. Social media is blamed today, and movies were blamed before that. The printing press was blamed before movies were invented, and rival priesthoods were blamed before printing was invented. People blame externals because it's hard to accept their internal status urge.

Mirror neurons alert us when others get rewards. Monkeys always notice the food and mating opportunities that other monkeys get. Nature equipped us to learn from others in our quest to meet our needs. Everyone keeps score, without consciously intending to. When you see someone get more rewards than you have, it grabs your attention. Thus you long for the fast lane without consciously intending to.

Each generation glamorizes the fast lane with the latest technology. In the eighteenth century, paperback books were suddenly mass-produced at a cheap price. Jane Austen devoured novels about fast-lane lives, and Sigmund Freud loved novels about Roman generals. Their elders cursed the new technology that filled their heads with this junk. But every young brain is eager for information on how to get ahead in the world.

We all learn from the information around us, so one person might buy a lot of shoes to feel important, while another feels important by looking down on people with a lot of shoes. Whatever we learn, the one-up feeling is soon metabolized and we want more. More shoes. More moral superiority. More visions of prestigious lovers or heroic generals. It seems reasonable because your brain sees others getting it.

To understand this feeling, imagine yourself spending the day in front of an ice cream shop. It seems like other people enjoy that creamy ecstasy all the time. Your mirror neurons give you the idea that you are missing out. Your inner mammal doesn't do statistics. So even if your rational brain knows better, you have the impression that other people eat ice cream all the time.

Your rational cortex does not make your decisions, even though it feels that way. Your two brains work together, but only your cortex reports to you in words. The cortex gathers data and feeds it to your mammal brain, which makes the final decision by releasing a happy or unhappy chemical. Then, your cortex has veto power. It can put on the brakes and start the whole process over by feeding more information to your mammal brain. Then, your verbal brain comes up with a "good" reason for the decision. You believe your verbal brain is the whole story if you don't understand your mammal brain.

We have to understand the animal urge for the fast lane in order to understand ourselves. Some animals reproduce a lot, some do not reproduce at all, and many are in the middle. A mammal is always trying to get ahead but also to avoid getting killed. An animal with an exaggerated sense of its own power is likely to get killed. That would not help spread its genes, so natural selection built a brain that weighs social risks against social rewards. We do this with pathways built from past experience, but since we learn from childhood experience, we can end up with an exaggerated sense of our own importance. Psychiatrists call it "grandiose delusions" when a person thinks they are Napoleon or Jesus. But how do we distinguish psychotic grandiosity from "big dreams"? A psychiatrist would say that the psychotic has lost touch with reality, but a performance coach or schoolteacher will tell you to imagine your own reality. Modern culture exhorts you to imagine huge triumphs, and it starts to feel real.

Of course, there is a difference between high performance and psychotic grandiosity. The high performer takes action that gets results. But in daily life, we see high performers getting rewards without seeing the effort and risk involved in getting those rewards. So the fast lane appears more rewarding and less painful than it actually is. Your mammal brain doesn't calculate discounted rates of return.

Sometimes you hear that a young person lit themselves on fire in order to win glory on the internet. In past generations, young people did painful things to win glory with whatever technology was available at the time. Experience wired their brains to expect the good feeling of glory to outweigh the bad feeling of self-destructive choices.

THE LURE OF THE SLOW LANE

The slow lane has a charm of its own. It helps you feel safe, so another martini seems fine.

The slow lane feels safe for a reason that may not be obvious to your conscious brain: You are safe from failure. You can't fail if you don't try. If you have tried and failed in the past, cortisol wired you to fear trying. You don't think this in words. You just avoid things you associate with the past failure. You can end up avoiding a lot.

When you were a child, adult status games had no meaning to you, but cortisol did. One-down feelings such as humiliation and shame are well-known childhood experiences. A little monkey perseveres despite the cortisol because it is hungry. But young humans are often rewarded whether they learn a skill or not. Sometimes, they even get extra rewards when they fall short in some way. Without the motivation of contingent rewards, avoiding cortisol may seem more attractive. The choice to prioritize pain avoidance over reward seeking builds a pathway that avoids pain instead of building for effective action. Children can get wired for failure when surrounded by well-intentioned efforts to protect them from pain.

The slow-lane habit can be learned in many different ways. Some children may fear trying because they were confronted by impossible challenges, while others may fear trying because they were overprotected. Children are not good judges of their long-term best interests. Bad feelings seem overwhelming to children because they don't know whether threats are real or not. Children need adult guidance to overcome the presumption that threatened feelings signal real threats. If parents do not provide that essential feedback, teachers might. But sometimes, there are no adults willing to give a child that essential real-world feedback. Thus, the child gets wired to avoid bad feelings at all costs instead of realistically weighing rewards and threats.

A person can learn to believe that doing nothing is the best choice. In the state of nature, doing nothing brings pain; but in the modern world, doing nothing avoids pain in the short run. You don't think this with your verbal brain, so it can be hard to know why you made this choice. But when you try to take action, cortisol surges and you revert to the pathways you have.

The slow lane protects you from pressure to try. It protects you from the fear of looking stupid when you fail to reach a goal. It protects you from jealousy and accusations of selfishness. The more you imagine people criticizing you, the more you like the shelter of the slow lane. Each time you relieve a threatened feeling by choosing the slow lane, you wire yourself to choose it again.

You suffer the downside to the slow lane, of course. You see other cars whizzing by and feel left behind. But no way to speed up looks safe, so you give up and order a pizza. For a few moments, the pizza distracts you from the one-down feeling.

Animals have a slow lane too. Weaker animals get protection from stronger animals as long as they submit. Weaker baboons don't face lions themselves; they let stronger baboons face the danger and cede food and mating opportunity in exchange.

You may be relying on stronger baboons to face lions for you. Maybe you resent them when you see them speed past you. Such conflicted feelings are hard to manage, but the slow lane helps you manage them. You surround yourself with others who have chosen it. They will always share a pizza with you.

BUILDING A HEALTHY SEROTONIN PATHWAY

You can enjoy serotonin in healthy ways. You can steer a middle path between too much pride and too little. The simple way to do this is to put yourself up without putting others down.

That's not easy, and the animal perspective helps us see why. Animals compete for resources because they cannot create resources. Humans can get rewards by creating resources instead of competing for them. Focusing on your creative power helps relieve your inner mammal's worries about losing resources to competitors. A village that knows how to plant has less reason to plunder.

You can feel one-up about your creation whether or not it gets recognition from others. You can learn to applaud your own steps instead of waiting for the world to applaud you. It would be nice to get a standing ovation from your fellow mammals, but if you expect that, you will feel disappointed a lot. That makes it harder to create.

You may notice yourself focusing on what your rivals are doing instead of on what you are creating. When they get ahead of you, you feel bad. Fortunately, you can stop the bad feeling by shifting your focus back to what you are creating. That's hard to do if you are wired to focus on rivals. You keep denigrating rivals even though it diverts energy from steps that can meet your needs. It feels good in the short run because you get the one-up position in a way that's familiar. But you can build new pathways to feel one-up without putting others down.

To do that, you have to feed your brain a new experience repeatedly. It's hard to do that because old pathways make your new thought seem foolish and unreliable. But each time you take pride in your creation, a trickle of serotonin rewards you. A new pathway builds if you keep returning your focus to the pride of what you are building instead of on "them."

If your pride depends on immediate recognition from others, you will miss out on serotonin. It's important to know that immediate recognition is rare. The great contributors of history often failed to get recognized until they were gone. When they did gain in status, it was often accompanied by vicious criticism. If people only did things that got immediate respect, we would not have the comforts we have today. Read biographies of people who developed the technologies that we now take for granted. You will see how much we benefit from the efforts of people who kept trying when they were ignored, ridiculed, and even attacked.

We would still be living in caves if people only did things that got immediate applause. If you need the world's applause to keep going, you won't get much done. Yet we are often told that others get rewards easily. The truth is that there is no reliable formula for getting recognition from your fellow mammal, so we must learn to keep going without it.

Take steps that you are proud of and your serotonin will flow. Your steps don't need to be colossal to get a drip of happy chemical. They can be modest as long as you follow them with a next step. Even when you fail, you can plan a next step that you are proud of and spark some serotonin. Dopamine will reward you when you see yourself meeting a need. Oxytocin will reward you when you find support along the way. You will wire in positive expectations about your next step. This is the motivational system that nature endowed us with.

HEALTHY STATUS VS. JUNK STATUS

Junk status is like junk food: it feels good now but hurts you later. Junk status can distract you from healthy status the way junk food distracts you from healthy food.

When others yield to junk status, you notice. You wonder why people waste their time on foolishness. But sneering at other people's junk status does not really help you in the long run. It just wires you to expect sneering from others. Berating the junk status of others is itself a form of junk status. You can learn to replace junk status with healthy status. You can respect the efforts of others, and thus train your brain to expect others to respect your efforts. That makes it easier to seek wholesome status in the long run.

It's tempting to feel one-up by denigrating others. It's even more tempting to denigrate rivals for the status you seek. When you find yourself frustrated with others, it helps to notice how they threaten your status. If you shift your focus toward putting yourself up instead of putting them down, you will enjoy more serotonin in the long run.

Healthy status seeking is a complex skill, but you can learn it the same way that you learn healthy eating. You may love junk food, but you build better habits when you learn about your nutritional needs. It's the same with status. You may love junk status, but you learn about your mammalian need for social importance, and build better habits to meet it.

We all have strong opinions about food, so it's nice that we get to make our own choices. It's the same with status. We have our own opinions about this complex need, so it's nice that we can choose our own way to seek it.

You can critique other people's diets all day, but your health depends on what you actually put in your mouth. It's the same with status. Your serotonin depends on your own steps toward healthy pride, even if the missteps of others seem glaringly obvious.

You may think others have healthier bodies because they got better genes, but you fail to account for their healthy choices. It's the same with status. You can jump to the conclusion that others got better sero-tonin genes without noticing their healthy thoughts about status.

An occasional indulgence in junk food will not ruin you, and it's the same with status. You can pull into the fast lane for an occasional treat, and then return to nourishment of the middle lane.

Some people eat healthy food, but they worry constantly about their food choices. This constant worry erodes the benefit of their good diet. It's the same with status. Some people stay reliably in the middle lane, but they worry endlessly about ending up in the slow lane. Their focus on threats erodes the pleasure of their healthy choices. We are meant to take pleasure in food, and it's the same with status. If you are on a healthy path, take pleasure in it instead of always worrying that it is not healthy enough. Sometimes the threat you fear is real, and you might have to act to protect yourself. But then you return to the middle lane instead of living in constant fear of status threats.

Healthy status comes from action. It's not enough to just dream of sta-tus. It's not enough to just avoid junk status. You have to define what you want to create and step toward it. Then you have to value what you've done instead of waiting for public recognition. You can master this skill with practice.

FINDING YOUR POWER

You may feel powerless when others do not give you the recognition you desire.

You have no power over other people's brains, so as long as you focus on them, you will feel powerless. To enjoy your own power, you need to focus on things you have control over, like taking a step that you're proud of.

For example, an Olympic medalist does not win by focusing on the ecstatic cheers of the crowd. They do not win by hating their competi-tors. They win by focusing on their daily practice routine. They take pride in their training regimen, and that triggers short-run serotonin. A big serotonin bonus could come with a future win, but that's so unpre-dictable that they need an alternative path to happiness. The point is not that you will win the gold if you don't think about it. The point is that you can feel good today by focusing on a step you are proud of.

What if you are already wired to focus on the glory of the finish line? You feel like you are missing something as you watch others getting applause. The more you focus on the rewards of others, the more one-down you feel. You can reverse that bad feeling right now by taking a step that you're proud of. A new pathway will build if you repeat that choice, and your thoughts will soon flow there as easily as they now dwell on the recognition that others are getting.

One-down feelings seem like facts about the world until you know how your pathways created them. Then you know that you can redirect your electricity into more powerful thoughts. You can do it in three simple steps:

1. Accept your mammalian urge for social importance.
2. Design small steps that you can be proud of and take them.
3. Repeat the new steps so a new pathway builds.

Here is a simple example: Imagine you're at a concert enjoying a great performance. The audience erupts with applause after a brilliant solo. It reminds you of your adolescent dream of musical greatness. You feel a sudden sense of disappointment, loss, emptiness, failure. The next morning, you still feel bad. This surprises you because you usually feel good after a concert. You could lift your mood with one of your usual feel-good habits, but you know that would not be good for you in the long run. So you decide to make peace with your inner mammal.

First, you acknowledge your deep longing for recognition. You realize that it feels urgent because your other needs are met, and the brain always focuses on the unmet need. Instead of criticizing yourself, or criticizing the world, you accept your natural mammalian impulse. You look for the old thought loop that is causing your sense of alarm. You have built a good life for yourself, but there are no moments of glory like wild appreciation you heard for last night's soloist. When you were young, you had a garage band, and you dreamed of greatness. In time, you let it go for more practical matters. You could go back to it, but you realize that it's not what you really want. The garage band was just a youthful way to feel independent. It got you out of the house and gave you decisions to make for yourself. You have achieved the independence that you longed for back then. You can honor yourself for that instead of needing the cheers of an audience. You used your garage-band dreams in a healthy way.

But it's not enough. You still feel a longing for recognition of some sort. Your adolescent dreams of glory are not a good guide for how to get it today, but that doesn't mean you should entirely reject the natural urge to feel special. As you look for a way to do that, you realize how much you have accomplished in your life. After your garage band failed, you invested your energy in useful pursuits, and you did well. Now you see the problem: Your brain has habituated to the rewards that you already have. You don't feel special because the things you have already accomplished feel so last-year. You need a new goal because you have achieved your earlier goals. The empty feeling comes from your achievement—not your lack of achievement.

You see how tempting it is to ignore your accomplishments and chase an adolescent dream. Suddenly, you are proud of yourself for recognizing this feeling instead of rushing to fill it in an old way. You accept your natural urge to feel special, but instead of expecting to meet it with big wins or dramatic moments of glory, you look for steps you can take every day. Tomorrow, for example, you are giving a presentation at work. The thought of it gives you a bad feeling, and suddenly you see the pattern: you expect to be criticized when you take the stage. Your music was criticized, and your first big presentation was criticized, so your brain is always looking for criticism. And now you see a bigger truth: you haven't prepared very well because you expect disappointment. You wonder if it could be different. You try to imagine yourself giving a great presentation and getting a great reception. But it doesn't work. You just can't picture it.

Then you see the problem. You can't change your brain overnight. You can easily imagine criticism of your presentation because you built up that pathway for years. You will see it through a negative lens until you build a positive lens. That will take small steps repeated often, so you decide to start stepping now. You invest energy in that presentation, and you feel proud of yourself, even though you can't control the reaction of others. You feel so good that you volunteer to do another presentation.

THE MODERN TABOO

When someone is called "self-important," it is usually meant as an insult. Ego is taboo in modern culture. You are expected to express pride in yourself without violating the ego taboo. This seems like an impossible conundrum, and the stakes are high because the penalty for ego is public derision. This makes it hard to get real about our own impulses.

But denying your impulses makes your inner mammal feel squelched. You think the world is squelching you because you don't see how you're doing it yourself.

A striking example of this inner conflict is the currently popular expression: "I'm so humbled." When people say this, they really mean "I'm so proud." They are getting the recognition they long for, but it's taboo to say that. You don't even dare to think it, because the rebuke would be so harsh if you let people see that you enjoy your moment of importance. So you pretend to feel one-down instead of one-up. "I'm so humbled" is the YouTube generation's version of the age-old primate status game.

The taboo on self-importance has value, of course. If everyone unleashed their one-up impulses, we'd have endless conflict. Humans train their children to restrain that natural impulse. This parenting strategy has been around for at least three millennia if we judge by the Ancient Greek tale of Icarus and Daedalus. Daedalus invented wings to help his son escape from prison, but warned his son not to fly too high because the sun would melt the wax holding the wings together. Icarus ignored his father's advice. The soaring felt so good that he kept going. Soon, he fell into the sea and drowned. The lesson is obvious: Moderating your urge to soar is a matter of life and death.

Today, many parents are reconsidering this message. They want their children to soar. Of course they also want their children to respect others. But parents want their children to have what they themselves lack, because the brain is always focused on the unmet need. Many parents have restrained their impulses in order to give their children a good life. Thus, they want to give their children freedom from self-restraint. For most of human history, parents grew up hungry and cold, so they dreamed of giving their kids enough food and warmth. Today, with our comfortable lives, we want to give our kids wings to fly to the sun.

Parents get vicarious pleasure from anticipating the future greatness of their children. They relieve the disappointment of their responsible moderation by telling their child to fly. But children often see this as a burden rather than a pleasure. They feel obliged to live fast-lane lives after growing up in the safety of the slow lane. They see the real risk of flying too high and drowning in the sea.

Our mammalian urge for status leaves us with an impossible double-bind. If you take this double-bind seriously, it can make you miserable in a life that is safer and more comfortable than any of your ancestors. But you have a choice. You can interpret your up-and-down feelings as blips on an ancient radar screen rather than as factual evidence of calamity. You can accept the reality of our ancient motivational mechanism. Instead of cursing your mammal brain, you can pride yourself on your ability to operate it.

THE STATUS GAMES OF MR. AND MRS. GIBBON

Madeleine and Mark Gibbon are high-profile members of their community. They manage a health care foundation and spend much of their time fundraising to keep it going. The Gibbons pass their days forcing smiles in meetings and receptions.

Madeleine inherited the foundation from her grandfather and grew it significantly. She and her husband are proud of their accomplishments, but also frustrated. They feel like they're on a treadmill. Their reasons are different, but they both hate to continue but also hate to stop.

Madeleine feels like she can't stop until they get the recognition they're due. She thinks their valuable contributions should be rewarded with certain milestones that have been denied to them so far. They have never received the annual award from their industry association, though they've done more for the industry than anyone, in Madeleine's opinion. They have not been invited to testify in congressional hearings, though they know more about the industry than anyone, Madeleine thinks. And she feels that their charitable works have not gotten the public attention they are due. If they stop now, they will miss out on the proper reward for all their effort.

Mark wants to continue because they run the organization better than anyone else could, in his opinion. They'd be letting the public down by turning things over to new management. Mark does not enjoy his workday very often, but he can't imagine himself doing anything else. Who would he be without it?

Madeleine and Mark feed each other's choice to stay on the treadmill.

Then, while driving home from an out-of-town meeting one day, they listen to an audiobook about the inner mammal. They slowly understand their natural concern for status. They look for patterns in their early experience that match their current feelings about status. Soon, it's all clear.

Madeleine grew up hearing about her grandfather's ambitions. She heard his pride, but she also heard his bitterness about being denied the recognition he thought he was due. She heard him venting a lot about competitors and administrators who blocked his path. But she loved being around him because he respected her, trained her, and put her into positions of authority. Suddenly, Madeleine sees how she absorbed his bitterness along with his competence. She is mirroring his distress. She can justify this with nice, rational arguments, of course. She has plenty to say about the clueless people who have stood in the way of her dreams for the foundation. But now she sees that distress will fill her life if she keeps letting her electricity flow into the old pathway. She decides to stop doing this now. She's not sure how, so she discusses it with Mark.

Mark cannot find the status-anxiety pattern in his early experience. He would rather not think about his early experience, in fact. But one day, at one of their many fundraisers, Madeleine sees a look on his face that reminds her of a one-down monkey she saw in a nature video. Suddenly, she sees his life in a different way. She and Mark are always putting themselves in a one-down position as they court donors and beg for money. Mark likes the status perks of the job, but his inner mammal is not fooled. It feels one-down most of the time. Madeleine is not sure if she should say this to him, so she makes popcorn and puts on a video about status seeking in monkeys.

Mark gets it. He remembers the way his mother was always trying to impress people. He hated listening to that, but he had no choice because his mother always dragged him into her status-seeking schemes. He promised himself he would never live that way. Has he broken that promise?

He sees how he drifted into status-seeking to support Madeleine. Sometimes he enjoyed it, and when it felt bad, he didn't know why. Now he sees the pattern: a natural mammalian fear of being a nobody, and on top of that, a fear of disappointing the woman in his life. He keeps running from this fear in the way he already knows: with half-hearted submission to someone else's quest.

The Gibbons decide that they are ready for something new, but they don't know what. Neither of them wants to retire to a life of frivolity because they don't think it would feel good. But they're not sure what would feel good. Their new knowledge suggests that they need new ways to feel strong and proud. And they know that new choices may feel wrong at first, and even dangerous, because old, myelinated pathways feel safe. So they decide to repeat a new choice until a new pathway builds and the new choice feels normal. But what new choice?

To Mark, every choice seems bad. He feels bad if he seeks status and bad if he doesn't. He thinks he's foolish and feels bad about that too. How could he have spent his life on such a hopeless mindset? But the more he thinks about it, the more he sees the foundation of his mindset. His mother had good reason to worry about status because his father did things that put the family at risk. To make matters worse, his parents competed for his loyalty. He hated being in the middle, but he didn't want to disappoint either one. He never spent much time developing his own source of pride.

Mark suddenly notices his habit of putting himself down. He decides to look for a more positive way to view his situation. He sees with relief that he made the best of a bad situation. He can feel smart for having done so much with his life instead of feeling dumb for being human. It feels good to give himself credit and he sees that it's a way to feel good in the future. He doesn't need to replace his old job with a giant mountain to climb. His dream is to have more variety in his life instead of chasing a big goal. He doesn't know where that will lead, but he sees that he can feel good without chasing something big.

Madeleine is not sure about her next step. Part of her wants to just delete the old template that tells her to court the goodwill of others. But part of her thinks that's crazy. You can't go through life not caring what anyone thinks, she says. She sees that Mark is enjoying a new freedom, and she gets mad at him. She starts to tell him why, but the words don't come. Usually, she's good at telling people what they are doing wrong, but it suddenly occurs to her that her judgment might be coming from an old pathway.

She searches her memory to excavate the pattern. Her grandfather often criticized others. It taught her to fear criticism, but also to be quick to criticize. She condemns herself for wanting more time off, so she condemns Mark for that too. She presumes it's wrong to take time off because she can't imagine that an old pathway could be causing her feelings. But when she looks for a good reason to condemn their new desires, she can practically feel herself sliding into an old loop. Self-criticism floods her mind, and the words and tone are eerily similar to those of her grandfather.

She realizes that she will spend her life running from imagined criticism unless she builds a new thought loop. She wishes she could just delete the old circuit, but then she remembers all the good things about her grandfather that might be lost with it. And she sees that he wanted her to be happy. That will be her new thought loop, she decides. Instead of filtering the world for threats of disappointing him, she will filter for the satisfaction he would have wanted for her. Her satisfaction may differ from Mark's, but they can support each other's choice to quit their old status game and take a chance on new ways to satisfy the natural urge to feel important.

Chapter Eight

Practical Steps toward Serotonin

You can find new steps toward serotonin with whatever brain you have. Start by recognizing your existing serotonin pathways and then open yourself to new sources of pride and strength. Status games will always tempt you because you will always be a mammal. Old pathways will always tempt you because they are so efficient. But you can blaze a new trail through your jungle of neurons despite those temptations. You can enjoy the good feeling of serotonin in ways that don't hurt you in the long run.

Here are stories of three people who did that. I call them Mr. Mandrill, Ms. Squirrel, and Mr. Vervet, after my favorite monkeys. They have very different lives, but they blazed their new trails in the same way: by accepting their mammalian urge for social importance, designing a new way to stimulate the good feeling, and repeating the new choice until it felt natural.

1. ACCEPT YOUR INNER MAMMAL

Mr. Mandrill's Story

Joe Mandrill likes to steal. He's good at it, and he feels proud of his skill.

He's getting out of jail today and would rather not go back. But stealing gives him a powerful feeling, so the idea of giving it up leaves him feeling bad.

Joe's probation officer asks what his plans are, and he can't think of anything. So he accepts an employment referral and is soon working as a busboy.

The first day at work is hard, but when Joe returns to his grandmother's apartment, he feels strangely good. He was around people all day, and they were surprisingly nice to him. Many people smiled at him, and he sort of froze because he wasn't used to it. Joe is thinking about smiling back tomorrow. Maybe.

A week goes by, and a new busboy is hired by the restaurant. Joe hates him at first. The new guy is tall and has a Hollywood face that would steal a man's lady in an instant. Joe catches the guy emptying a tray the wrong way, and he's sure the guy is an idiot. But the guy smiles at him, so Joe walks over and shows him the right way. The guy smiles again, and Joe feels curiously good.

The next day, the boss asks Joe to help train the new guy. A week later, Joe is promoted to kitchen assistant. He feels great and can't wait to tell his grandmother.

But the first day in the kitchen is awful. They give him a lot of instructions at once, and he's terrified of making a mistake. He's sure the chef wants to catch him in a mistake, and that makes him really mad. The bad feeling is so intense that he can hardly focus on the onion he's chopping. Then, the chef says his chopped onion looks good, and he's suddenly ecstatic. He notices how quickly he can go from bad feelings to good. And he's surprised at how quickly the bad feeling comes back when they move him from onions to garlic. He waits for the chef to tell him he got it right so he can relax. But the chef is busy with something else, so he's challenged to live with the bad feeling a bit longer.

Break time comes, and as Joe walks from the kitchen to the break room, he passes a freezer with a big lock on it. He knows that lock! He could pick it in a minute! That old pride wells up in him. Of course, he wouldn't do it now. So many people are around.

Once Joe gets back to work, he happens to glance toward the lock on the freezer. A good feeling comes on and relieves his fear of failure for a moment. The next time he worries about making a mistake, he looks toward the lock. It works! He can't explain it, but it's nice to have a reliable way to feel good when he needs it.

A week later, Joe has the opportunity to work overtime. That results in him being alone near the lock for the first time. He doesn't know what's in the locked-up freezer, but he can't stop thinking about it. A rush of excitement takes over his tired body. The feeling is quite familiar.

The next morning, Joe wakes up with a memory of his first lock-picking experience. When he was only twelve years old, his cousin, "Big Joe," brought him along on a job. He was thrilled to be included, and even more thrilled when Big Joe started teaching him "the family business." Joe was over the moon with pride when his cool older cousin praised his skill.

At break time that day, Joe puts his hands on the lock when he passes it. He feels the old familiar thrill.

A line cook calls in sick, and Joe Mandrill is asked to fill in. He learns how to make the house-specialty omelet in three minutes flat. He feels terrified at first, but by the end of the lunch shift, he's bursting with pride at his creations. As he leaves for the day, he passes the lock and realizes that he hasn't thought about for in hours. And he's amazed to see that he got the same feeling from omelets.

Ms. Squirrel's Story

Janet Squirrel is losing her husband and her job at the same time. She can't understand how this could happen after all she did for them. She kept everyone marching at work and at home, and instead of being grateful, they're abandoning her.

Jan felt sick when her boss gave her the news. She went home and stayed in bed for two days. Now, her boss is asking when she'll be back—she was not actually fired, she realizes—it just felt that way because she was demoted. A new layer of management was added above her, and the job was given to a woman from outside the company. Jan feels devastated, but she tries to pull herself together to keep the job. She tells the boss she'll be there in the morning.

But the next morning, her estranged husband calls. He wants to pick up some stuff because he's been living out of a suitcase since she kicked him out. How dare he say that she kicked him out! He left. It was right after she told him to leave if he couldn't mend his ways. Their conversation upsets her so much that she calls in sick.

She lies in bed thinking, "How dare he!" over and over. She doesn't fully understand the bad feeling that overcomes her. But the feeling is strangely familiar. Suddenly, she remembers her mother saying, "How dare you" over and over. When Jan was twelve, her father left, and her mother stayed in bed. Jan took care of her younger siblings because her older siblings were never home. She sent the little ones to school clean and fed every day, with their homework finished. She was proud of the way she kept them marching, though she never got any recognition for it. Her mother found lots to criticize, often erupting with, "How dare you!"

Jan went from that struggle to managing a big staff at work and raising a family of her own. She's still proud of her ability to keep people marching. But her kids are on their own now, and her boss and husband don't appreciate her. How dare they!

Jan can hardly move, so she thinks she may have a neurological disorder. She searches for information, and after reading in bed for hours, she stumbles on information about the mammal brain. But she doesn't agree with what it says.

"I don't care about status," she insists, though she can see that others clearly do care about status. She keeps reading, and when hours have passed, she notices that she feels curiously better. She gets a good night's sleep, and in the morning, she can't wait to learn more about her inner mammal. She calls in sick again.

Janet Squirrel starts to see the fear she felt as a child when her parents retreated, and how those fear pathways are still with her. She hates to admit this. Fear is stupid, she thinks, and old fear is worse. But when she learns that it's natural, she can accept herself and relax. She had good reason to feel unsafe as a child. She can be proud of the way she learned to feel strong in a bad situation. And she can learn to focus on her strength instead of her weakness.

That will take time, she realizes. And she needs to make peace with her boss and her husband sooner than that. She feels strong enough to start, so she messages both of them to set up meetings.

Mr. Vervet's Story

Al Vervet is having heart palpitations. His girlfriend says he should go to the doctor, but he refuses. The last doctor asked him nosy questions and ignored Al's perspective. Al knows why he has heart problems. He is very compassionate, and his big heart goes out to everyone, so it gets a big workout. Al is proud of his empathy, so he wouldn't change a thing.

Al is in a hurry to end this conversation with his girlfriend because he has a date with his new woman. He has been with Number Two for over a year, but he still thinks of her as "new." He tells Number One that he has to leave for a work commitment, and she shouldn't worry because his heart will settle as soon as he smokes a joint. He lights up, and when he passes it to her, he sees her disappointment at his leaving. But he's too compassionate to break up with her, so it will have to be this way. Number Two accepts this as well. And if she complains, he has his eye on the perfect replacement. He only wants love in his life, not anger.

When he arrives at Number Two's place, she suggests a walk in the park. Al's heart palpitations start again, but he doesn't say anything. In the park, they see people playing chess. Al's chest tightens as he remembers playing chess with his older brother. Jim would fly into a rage if he lost, so Al would lose to keep the peace. It didn't really work because Jim would find something else to get mad at.

Suddenly, Al is lying on the ground looking up at paramedics. He must have passed out. They insist on taking him to the hospital. Soon, he's hooked up to machines and has nothing to do but think. The chess game drifts back to his mind.

Texts start arriving. Number Two wants to visit him in the hospital. Number One wants to plan for tomorrow. He tenses up as he calculates his next move. It feels like a chess game. Why am I playing this game? he wonders. But he concludes that he has no choice because he's too kind to hurt anyone.

A doctor walks in and says, "Good news. There's no evidence of an organic problem. Have you been under stress?" He advises Al to reduce stress however possible.

Al explodes at the doctor and explains his big-hearted theory of palpitations. The doctor nods politely and walks out.

Al Vervet is humiliated. He never attacked a doctor before. "I sounded like my brother and father," he thinks. He starts to plan an apology. Then, it occurs to him that apologizing is like a move in a game. It doesn't change anything. Al will still have heart palpitations. He will still be the "big-hearted" guy who pretends to be "nice." He thinks of researching "heart palpitations," but he writes the words "too nice" in the search bar instead. One thing leads to another and he ends up reading about his inner mammal. Suddenly, everything makes sense!

Al Vervet sees how he got wired to anticipate attack. He is always defending himself from the attack he expects. Sometimes he defends by being "nice," and other times he mounts an attack himself. He tries to cover these attacks with "nice," so he doesn't feel like a jerk. Either way, he is always fearing the next attack. It puts a strain on him. He wants to give his inner mammal another way to see the world.

2. DESIGN A HEALTHY PATH TO PRIDE

Mr. Mandrill's Story

Joe Mandrill is excited to tell his grandmother about his triumph as a line cook. He wants to tell her the even better story about how he learned to control his feelings, but he stops in mid-sentence because mentioning the lock would get his cousin in trouble. So even as his grandmother says she's proud of him, he knows there's something more to be proud of. He has mastered his brain!

The next day, Joe has a new bounce in his step. But when he enters the kitchen, he sees that the line cook is back. Joe's opportunity is gone. He feels horrible.

But it's a new kind of horrible, he notices. In the past, he would have felt like screaming and breaking into the freezer. Now, he's mostly thinking about how to get a job as a line cook. He doesn't know how, though, so he still feels bad.

When Joe gets home, his grandmother is sick in bed. He doesn't know what to do, so he offers to make dinner. He makes her an omelet, and he's surprised by how good he feels while he's doing it. That night, he checks out the cooking channel instead of the sports channel. He's so mesmerized that hours go by before he notices.

The next day, he decides to just ask the chef for a promotion to line cook. But when he opens his mouth, he's frozen with fear. It's the same feeling he has when he hears a police siren during a robbery. He decides to ask tomorrow. He goes home disappointed and puts on the cooking channel.

As he watches, he decides to cook something. He's thrilled with the beautiful casserole he makes and decides to share it at work at lunch time. As he's passing it around, the chef walks by. Joe Mandrill rushes over to offer him some and blurts out his request for promotion. The chef says there are no openings right now, but Joe will be first in line when there is one.

Ms. Squirrel's Story

Janet Squirrel is nervous about her meetings with her boss and her husband. She doesn't know how to make things right. In the past, she would have just taken charge, but that didn't work out so well. How can she do things differently?

She wants to tell her boss that he's making a huge mistake with this new hire. Part of her thinks she shouldn't say this. But part of her thinks that you have to tell someone when they're going wrong. You can't just let them drive over a cliff. It's common decency!

She wants to tell her husband that he's making a huge mistake by moving out. She knows how badly he will do without her. She just wants to protect him from going over a cliff.

Suddenly, Jan sees the pattern. She imagines people going over cliffs all the time. She fears going over cliffs herself if she lets others make decisions. She wants to save everyone from the disasters she thinks will happen. But she sees how she learned this from past experience.

When Jan was young, there were a lot of disasters. She learned to manage them because she couldn't trust anyone else to do it. But as soon as she fixed one disaster, another came along. She has spent her whole life putting out fires.

"What else could I do?" she thinks. "I can't let everyone burn." Jan is stuck. She doesn't see how anything could be different. But the specter of divorce and unemployment motivate her to keep looking for a solution. She decides to watch some inner-mammal videos.

Now things are clearer. Our brain evolved to scan for threats, and we all learn to manage threatened feelings in whatever way worked before. Taking charge worked when Jan was young. She learned to see herself as the rescuer. Now, she has to be behind the wheel or she's sure the car will go over the cliff. It feels real because the circuit built up from real experience, and the chemicals are real right now. But others have their own circuits that feel equally real to them. She sees how her need for control could annoy colleagues, family, and even the siblings she hardly sees any more. They're all mammals, she thinks. They don't like being one-down, and they know she will take over if she's there.

She feels humiliated. How could she have let this go on for so long?

She doesn't know what to do so she makes a cup of coffee and watches another inner-mammal video. Finally, she sees the big picture. Nothing is wrong with me! I have strengths and weaknesses like everyone. I can take pride in my strengths and rewire my weaknesses.

She recognizes her strengths. She's efficient, proactive, and cares about others. She's open to new information. And she really is good at putting out fires.

Now for the rewiring. She knows she should target one new behavior at a time since it takes so much repetition. She decides to start with the big one: how to feel safe without taking control. She starts immediately by agreeing to the meeting times and places that her boss and husband suggest, even though she had some better ideas. She is proud of herself already.

Mr. Vervet's Story

Al Vervet is excited about the idea that he can rewire his brain. He wants to rewire his muscles too because he feels tight, like he's wearing a corset. He knows he should feed his brain new experiences—but what? How can he train his inner mammal to feel safe and strong?

Challenge his brother to a chess game!

He doesn't have to lose on purpose and squelch his resentment. He can play for real and manage his fear of his brother's anger. He knows that his old pathways may trigger the old fear, despite his good intentions. But he will be ready to respond in a new way. He will start feeding his brain with activities that give him a strong feeling, like playing the guitar and carpentry projects. He still feels bad when he thinks about challenging his brother, but he will not give his brain a chance to dwell on threatened feelings.

So from his hospital bed, Al calls his brother and invites him to play. They make a plan, and ten minutes later Jim calls back to change the plan. Al's cortisol revs up, so he has an immediate chance to practice his new plan. He tries to think of a feel-good activity he can do from a hospital bed. Just then, his phone rings. Number One wants to visit. He tells her to bring a chess set.

Al enjoys their game of chess, and prides himself on his indifference to winning or losing. But to be honest, he is winning right now, so he may need to test that theory again. Number One suggests a rematch after she loses, but Al is in a hurry to get rid of her because Number Two might show up. He says he needs to rest.

She insists on sharing a joint before she leaves, and when she lights up, a smoke alarm is triggered. A nurse walks in and asks her to put it out. She tells the nurse it's a stupid rule, and she is quickly escorted to the door by Security. She floods Al with angry texts, insisting that he fight for her. He doesn't really want to, but he doesn't want to say that. The texts get angrier and angrier. Al's chest tightens and his heart races. How can he escape this mess? He imagines himself moving to another country and starting over with a new identity.

But he sees that running away would not change anything, because he would still have the same pathways. He will keep creating the same mess as long as he fears other people's anger. He used to blame the mess on others, but now he sees how he creates it himself by making commitments that he doesn't intend to keep. He avoids conflict by agreeing to things he doesn't agree with. That's why he's always busy squirming out of things. He even remembers doing that as a kid. Though he prides himself on avoiding conflict, he does it by being deceitful. Thus, he's forever struggling to untangle a chain of deceptions. The insincerity has cost him jobs and friendships over the years, but no one said it to his face, so he never saw the pattern. He thought he was Mr. Smooth.

Al feels humiliated. The pattern is so pervasive when he sees it that he hardly knows where to start. A doctor walks in while he's lying there feeling miserable. "I hope you can fix me," Al says. The doctor checks his chart and says, "You're looking good. I'm releasing you."

Al Vervet is shocked. How did his heart get better while he was feeling worse? What now? Part of him wants to call his girlfriends to pick him up and go with whoever shows up first. Part of him wants to hide in a sanatorium on a mountain. But he sees the pattern now. He knows what he needs to do.

He will choose his next step instead of agreeing to steps pushed by others. When he doesn't know what to choose, he will wait until he is sure of his own mind instead of yielding to whomever pushes the hardest. His fear will still be there, but instead of yielding to it, he will look for a step he is proud of. He starts by paying for a ride home instead of calling someone.

3. REPEAT UNTIL A PATHWAY BUILDS

Mr. Mandrill's Story

Joe Mandrill thinks of looking for a job in another restaurant instead of waiting for an opening where he is. But when he thinks of doing that, he feels a police siren inside him. In the past, he would have turned off the siren by watching TV or hanging with his cousin. But now, he sees that things can be different. He can shift bad feelings to good feelings in new ways. So when he passes a restaurant on the way home from work, he walks in and asks for a job as a line cook.

They don't need one, alas. Joe's heart races as he hears the words. He thinks of all the reasons they don't want him. In a fog of shame, he wanders into a supermarket on his way home. He imagines himself cooking a big dinner and starts buying ingredients. He invites Big Joe, and tells him to bring some girls. By the time they arrive, Joe has shifted from shame to pride.

At work the next day, he hears coworkers chatting about past jobs at other restaurants. He realizes that everyone has lived through the agony of applying for jobs. If they can do it, he can too. He did it yesterday, he thinks with pride. So he decides to ask for a job at one restaurant every day. That will protect him from feeling like his whole life depends on any one person.

A week later, he has found the job of his dreams! He feels great for a few hours, but he's surprised how quickly the good feeling turns to fear. It's strange how he thought he'd be happy forever if he became a cook, but now all he can think about is making a mistake. He imagines himself doing everything right and becoming a head chef, but that only increases his fear of messing up and losing it all. He needs to practice calming down, so he decides to plan another dinner for his cousin and those girls.

When he calls Big Joe, he gets a huge shock. "You're wasting your time in restaurants. Come do a job with me. Tonight! " Joe tries to explain that he's happy with the path he's on, and his cousin makes a long string of nasty comments.

Joe feels devastated. Part of him wants to avoid his cousin forever, and another part of him wants to call back and say whatever it takes to make Big Joe happy.

Joe realizes how much he wants support. He wants the protection of someone bigger and stronger. He didn't get much support when he was young, which is why he followed his cousin so eagerly. Now, he sees that he is actually stronger without Big Joe. He feels foolish for wanting support so much, but he feels proud of seeing the difference between real support and fake support.

Then he realizes that dinner with his cousin was an excuse to see the girl, and he could just call the girl himself. He is scared as he finds her number, but he remembers his success in finding a new job. He thinks, "Maybe I'll ask a different girl for dinner each night so I don't worry too much about any particular one." But as soon as she says yes, he forgets about that.

Ms. Squirrel's Story

Janet Squirrel has learned to notice herself creating disaster scenarios. She is amazed at how often she flows into that template without consciously choosing it. She wants to give herself a more positive template to flow into. She considers applauding herself every time she lets go of a disaster scenario. But it doesn't actually feel good. She feels lazy and irresponsible when she lets go, as much as she wishes it were otherwise.

Then she remembers her inner mammal. It wants to feel a one-up position, and disaster management was her reliable way to do that. So she needs to give herself a healthy new one-up strategy to replace the old unhealthy one. Though she longs to be king of the hill, she realizes that's not the answer. Her mammal brain will just keep looking for a bigger hill and worrying about losing the hill it has.

The answer is to feel valuable in small ways instead of with big drama. Small moments are enough to feel good as long as she repeats them often. She decides to recognize her value three times a day for forty-five days. She knows the repetition will build a new pathway to feel valued without the need for drama. She will give herself a treat every day that she honors this commitment to herself. It seems fake, but if pigs can be trained to find truffles this way, she can train herself to feel good this way. It's not logical, but she has learned that her brain does not run on pure logic.

It works! Jan learns to feel dominant without actually dominating. She builds positive associations for her own actions so she can feel good without rescuing people from imagined disasters. She gives the electricity in her brain a new place to flow.

Mr. Vervet's Story

Al Vervet is hungry when he arrives home, but he can't decide what to eat. It scares him to realize that he left decisions to others so often that he cannot choose a meal without a push from someone. He'd like to call this proof of his caring nature, but he sees the problem. He wired himself to think he's a good person when he's accommodating others. So now he needs someone to accommodate in order to function.

The thought of asserting his own needs fills him with fear. Even when no one is there to assert to, thinking about his own needs scares him. He expect others to meet his needs for him, he realizes. He accommodates others because he wants to be accommodated in return. That's okay sometimes, but not as a primary way to meet your needs. Al sees how he manipulates others to meet his needs instead of doing things for himself. He sees that it's just a habit, but it's a deep habit.

Worst of all, Al sees that he feels wronged when others fail to guess his needs, and thus free to lie and manipulate. He doesn't think this in words, but he has been thinking it as far back as he can remember. He used to think people were annoying, but now he sees how he annoyed himself by anticipating conflict and running from it.

Al hates himself for being stuck in this thought loop. But he reminds himself that every brain relies on old thought loops. And every brain tries to feel special, so if he gives up his old way of feeling special, he has to give himself a new way. What can it be?

With his hunger growing, Al realizes that he can take pride in his ability to meet his own needs. He goes to a supermarket to buy food. But he has trouble making decisions. Is he buying for one person or two? One day or many? He checks his phone. Then, he realizes what he is doing. He is looking for someone to pressure him to do something so he can play the "nice guy" instead of making a decision. He's ashamed of himself.

But he forgives himself again, and reminds himself that it takes a lot of repetition to build a new pathway. Instead of putting himself down, he is proud of himself for noticing the impulse before he acts on it. Hunger is nature's core motivator. Al tells himself that any decision is better than defaulting to his old pattern. He buys enough food to work at home alone for the next two days.

Once he has eaten, Al knows he must reckon with his girlfriends. He is not sure what to say as he scrolls through the mass of messages. He notices the old temptation—to make soothing speeches and then negotiate. But he knows where that will lead. He will just agree to their demands and tell himself that he has a big heart. Maybe he even likes them fighting over him. The problem is that he hasn't made a decision in his own mind, so yielding to pressure will substitute for plotting a course. He must decide. He doesn't know what the decision will be, but he has decided to decide. Any decision will help build the new pathway instead of reinforcing the old one.

He composes a letter explaining that he needs to be alone for a while. He doesn't know how long, so they should move on without him. Then he turns off his phone. He literally powers down so he cannot be tempted to check the barrage of messages he expects. He will force himself to see the world through his own lens instead of seeing it through their reflections. He thinks about what he will have for breakfast tomorrow, and how much work he will catch up on. When his workday is over, he's not sure what he will do, but he will make the decision with pride.

The next morning, he yields to temptation just a little. He checks how many messages he has without actually reading them. Then he goes back to the course he has set.

The following morning, he checks his message count again. There are fewer messages. Al notices his reaction. He fears being alone if they actually give up on him. He's scared. Part of him wants to encourage both of them to keep pursuing him.

Al is shocked by how easily he slips into that old thought loop. He applauds himself for noticing the loop and shifts back to the new path he's building. He gets a lot of work done, and in the evening he makes plans for a home repair project and a solo vacation. He feels like the corset around him has loosened.

YOUR STORY

You can take pleasure in your own strength while respecting the strength of others.

You can give your inner mammal healthy ways to feel good.

You can rewire in new loops instead of defaulting to old loops.

It won't happen on its own. It won't happen by following the popular crowd. It will happen if you accept your natural urge to feel strong, find a healthy way to achieve that, and repeat it a lot.

It's hard to get real about your inner mammal because your verbal brain is so good at explaining things in ways that make you look good.

It's hard to get real because you've learned to blame others for status seeking instead of noticing your own impulses.

It's hard to find alternative ways to feel strong and important. There are no guaranteed paths to the one-up position, and every one-up moment passes quickly. The uncertainty is frustrating, so the brain falls back on past experience. You try to dominate in situations where that worked before and submit where that worked before. But the serotonin treadmill remains. To keep feeling it, you must take pride in your steps instead of expecting pride to be thrust on you when you reach the next peak.

It's hard to repeat a new thought or behavior. It doesn't feel comfortable the way your old habit does, so why would you want to repeat it? Cortisol fills you with fear when you leave old trails and explore new ones. You expect to relieve cortisol by being one-up, but as soon as you achieve that desired position, you start to fear losing it. You might soothe your fear by seeking protection from others, but that puts you in the one-down position and you fear being dominated. Your old cortisol pathways are powerful. But you can keep redirecting your attention from the old pathway to the new one.

It takes a lot of energy to activate a new neural pathway. You can do it if you focus your energy on the challenge instead of frittering it away on other things. Rewiring your brain is like learning a new language in adulthood: It's hard, but it's possible. People do it all the time. You will do it if you follow these steps:

1. Recognize and accept your mammalian thought loops instead of believing that your verbal inner voice is the whole story.

2. Design an alternative that puts you up without putting others down or needing their approval.
3. Repeat your new thought loop by finding a way to make it fun so you keep doing it.

It's casy to play status games and blame others for your choices, but you have power over your brain.

Chapter Nine

Help Others Escape Status Games

You may know people who are suffering from status games. Maybe you counsel, manage, or teach people who are suffering from status games. You may want to help.

There are good reasons to help, but there are also bad reasons.

"Helping" is a fast, easy way for you to feel one-up. You don't think this consciously, but you naturally feel stronger when you help someone who's weaker. You enjoy asserting yourself in the name of others if it feels dangerous to assert for yourself. And you relieve threatened feelings when you focus on someone else's threats.

So when you feel weak or threatened, you may rely on "helping" to give you a lift.

This would be fine if the "help" really helps. But sometimes it doesn't, and it can even make things worse. You won't notice if you need to "help" to meet your own needs. You will keep "helping" when it makes things worse because it still feels good to you. Thus, you must know whether you're helping for the wrong reasons.

It's wrong to use "help" as a substitute for getting real with your own brain. It's wrong to fix others because you can't fix yourself.

If you rely on helping to feel good, it's effectively your drug of choice. You are addicted to helping in the sense that you use it to feel better in the short run without regard to long-run consequences. We often overlook the true impact of "help" because it feels so good now.

We often try to manage other people's emotions because we can't manage our own.

No one likes to admit this.

It's easier to confront other people's status games than to confront your own. That makes it easy to overlook the possibility that your "help" is like buying candy for a diabetic. When you buy the candy, you feel good, so you want to do it again. Our illusions about serving others are not reliable guides to the greater good.

It's natural to want to help someone in pain, of course. But your perception of their pain may be mistaken. We project our own pain onto others more than we realize. Our brain is always scanning for potential threats, so when you see others in situations that threatened you before, your cortisol turns on. You can call it empathy, and applaud yourself for feeling their pain. But you may be exaggerating their pain, and even teaching them to get rewards by showing pain. This kind of "help" doesn't help.

If you are addicted to "helping," your verbal brain finds a way to make it sound good. You might even glorify the person you are helping. You say they are a magnificent tower of strength and they are really helping you. But beneath your fine words, your inner mammal is meeting its need for one-up feelings, so it wants to "help" more.

Thus, this chapter begins with a strong warning: Do not try to "help" until you have done the work yourself. If you are using "help" as a substitute for relieving your own status anxiety, reread the prior chapters before you read on. The person you want to help will learn from your actions more than your words. If you try to fix them instead of managing your inner mammal, you will teach them to focus on fixing people instead of taking responsibility for their own emotions.

This chapter is short because our ability to help is limited. You cannot reach into someone's brain and rewire them. What you can do is

- model the behavior you want others to learn;
- reward the behavior you want rather than the behavior you don't want;
- teach the facts about the mammal brain.

First, let's return to the monkey world for a fresh look at "help."

A NATURAL VIEW OF HELP

Monkeys don't get help. A monkey only eats nuts if it cracks one open itself. Not even your mother cracks nuts for you in the monkey world.

Monkeys desperately want to eat nuts because it meets their need for protein and fat. These nutrients create the muscles and rich milk necessary for reproductive success. Protein and fat are scarce in a rain forest diet, so if you don't learn to crack nuts, your genes will be wiped off the face of the earth. Yet cracking nuts is so hard that many monkeys fail for years. It's a lot of pressure.

When a monkey fails, it tries again. It watches what others are doing and mirrors them. If it crumbled in frustration its genes would not survive. We cannot be descended from monkeys who crumbled in frustration. We are descended from monkeys who persevered.

What would happen if you "helped" a monkey by giving it bags of pre-shelled nuts that it could eat while sitting on the couch? It would not learn essential survival skills. It would learn to pressure you for more nuts. And when it had enough, it would look for other ways to stimulate good feelings since it didn't stimulate them by taking steps to meet its needs.

MODEL BEHAVIORS THAT HELP

Our mirror neurons track the rewards and pain of those around us. When you enjoy rewards or suffer pain, others learn from that. They learn to seek what they see you enjoy and avoid what brings you pain. The rewards and pain you model influence others in a way that your words cannot.

I discovered the power of mirror neurons by accident. My dentist told me to floss "or else," but I couldn't get myself to do it. It seemed so hard that I couldn't even imagine anyone doing it. Then I met my husband and saw him floss every night in the most casual, relaxed way. Suddenly I saw that this was possible, so I tried again. It was still hard, but I persisted because I understood that it could get easy with repetition. Nothing was said in words, and I didn't even realize that I had learned in this way until I read about mirror neurons in a book.

We mirror emotional skills in the same way as physical skills. You help others learn healthy serotonin skills by modeling them yourself. If you feel strong and important without putting others down, the mirror neurons around you will pick it up. If you enjoy small steps instead of worrying about distant mountaintops, others will learn to enjoy small steps. If you manage disappointment without acting like your survival is threatened, you will help others manage disappointment.

Mirror neurons are weak compared to myelinated neurons. They only activate a subtle flow of electricity, unlike the gush we get from old pathways. But there's a positive side to this. Old pathways filter out so many inputs that even the subtle input of mirror neurons is noticeable. Mirror neurons get under the radar of our filters. We don't know we have filters until someone else's rewards or pain snags our attention. This is why bad models have power, and why good models are so valuable. By modeling healthy pride, you can help someone find alternatives that their junk-status pathways would have ignored.

The brain doesn't mirror everything. It only mirrors rewards and pain. So let others see the pleasure you get from your healthy serotonin strategy. You can even share your pain when you yield to junk status. If sharing personal experience is not appropriate in your context, you can introduce other healthy models. And you can find appropriate personal examples if you look. Here is a simple example. When I take my daily walk, I notice my neighbors' beautiful fruit trees. I do not have fruit trees, and I think how nice it would be to have them. But I know they would require a huge investment of effort that I am not willing to make. So instead of feeling bad about my lack of fruit trees, I admire what my neighbors have, and I admire what I've done with the time and energy I have invested elsewhere. This trains my mind to see a world in which people admire each other's creations. If I resented my neighbors' one-up position, I would see a world in which people resent each other's successes.

The dark side of mirror neurons must be recognized. When you help others, you anticipate their pleasure, and you mirror that pleasure. The good feeling motivates you to keep "helping" whether or not it helps. Parents often enjoy giving their children big rewards even when it doesn't help the child. Teachers and managers may enjoy giving big rewards whether or not it helps their students and colleagues in the long run. Mirror neurons make the temptation hard to resist.

I learned about the dark side of mirror neurons the hard way. When I was in college, I was trained to believe that a "helping" career was the only good path. I took a job in Africa with the United Nations. While I was there, I was shocked to learn that a huge chunk of foreign aid is stolen, and aid workers look the other way to protect their careers. This "help" made things worse because the rewards of stealing aid money are so much higher the rewards of than honest work. I decided to find a new career instead of focusing on "help."

The mammal brain expects reciprocity. A monkey who gives a grooming expects a benefit in return. We expect a benefit when we help, such as recognition that raises your status, social alliances that bring protection, and even karma points that boost your love life. You don't always get the benefits you expect, alas. This leaves you disappointed and you might use bad feelings as an excuse to make bad choices. You end up modeling bad choices despite your good intentions. You would do more good if you got real about your mammalian expectation of reciprocity.

It's tempting to assert yourself in the name of others because asserting for yourself feels taboo. When you claim to speak for "the little guy," you get to disgorge the disappointment, distress, and anger you feel for your own sake. But when you do this, you are modeling anger, not the peace of serotonin.

DON'T REWARD STATUS GAMES

This may seem obvious, but people often reward bad behavior, and thus train others to repeat the bad behavior. To help, you must carefully reward the desired behavior, and scrupulously avoid rewarding junk status. This is harder than it seems, for so many reasons:

- **Romanticized view of the mammal brain.** You may think you can win over an uncooperative individual with generous rewards. You assume they will be "nice" if you are "nice." But the mammal brain doesn't work that way. It learns from rewards. If you reward bad behavior, the brain learns to repeat bad behavior. So if you really want to help, you must carefully monitor the incentive structure you create. This includes intangibles like attention and respect as well as formal status and resources.
- **Fear of conflict.** We often reward bad behavior out of fear of retaliation by a stronger monkey. When you yield to this fear, you teach

everyone watching that bad behavior gets rewarded. You cannot help people until you can manage your own fear of conflict. Target the healthy steps you plan to reward, and withhold rewards until you see those steps.

- **Variable reinforcement or intermittent rewards.** If you reward bad behavior occasionally, you may think it couldn't do much harm. But animal research shows that intermittent rewards have more impact than predictable rewards. An animal will invest more effort to get a reward that only comes occasionally than it invests in a reliable reward. In the human world, well-known examples of variable reinforcement schedules are slot machines and giving in to a child's tantrums. When a person isn't sure when rewards will come, they try and try and try. So if you want to help, never reward status games, ever.

Our brain evolved to learn from carrots and sticks. But in the modern world, sticks are taboo, so we have lost half of our natural guidance mechanism. When you can't punish bad behavior, you try to manage with carrots alone. Imagine a horse who is given more and more carrots when it refuses to heed the trail. The horse soon loses interest in the carrots and roams where it wants to. Now imagine a person with an undesirable attention-seeking or dominance-seeking habit. You try to help by being extra "nice," but you may end up reinforcing their expectation that attention-seeking or dominating behavior will bring rewards. And everyone around you sees the dysfunctional incentive structure you have created. They know in a nonverbal way that you will take good behavior for granted and reward bad behavior.

Dysfunctional incentive structures are surprisingly common in human groups. At work, in schools, and in families, we often reward undesirable behaviors without intending to. I did it myself as a college professor. Many students cheated, and the culture among my fellow professors was to do nothing about it. This effectively rewarded bad behavior. Fancy theories about "help" were used to justify this, but in time I realized that it did more harm than good. I decided to take responsibility for my own incentive structure. I only gave grades for honest work instead of yielding to my fear of conflict. But young people still get rewarded for bad behavior a lot, and it's often done in the name of "help."

When you see a person falling short in some way, it's natural to want to give them a hand. But when a person gets recognition by failing, it trains their brain to get recognition by failing. No conscious intent is involved. If the person gets recognition by succeeding, they will be motivated to succeed rather than to fail. You can help a person get recognition by succeeding.

Little monkeys are never given solid food. They get nothing to eat except mother's milk unless they get it themselves. They will starve to death if they don't learn the skills necessary to meet their survival needs. Yet every monkey figures it out because the brain learns from rewards.

If you want to help, you must create a sound incentive structure. Identify the behaviors you want to reward and stick to your plan. It's easier when you remember that the brain is always learning from rewards.

GETTING REAL ABOUT OUR INNER MAMMAL

Few people know the facts about the mammal brain because a romanticized view of nature is popular. It lures you to think effortless happiness is our natural default state, and unhappiness is caused by "our society." This mindset is so pervasive that people have trouble thinking otherwise. That makes it hard to understand the one-down feelings that trouble us, and the status games we play to feel better. With more knowledge about our mammal brain, people can manage their serotonin with fewer status games.

It's hard for people to accept the fact that their brain strives for social importance, because we fear being condemned for selfishness. Instead, we insist that we only care about the greater good. But with patience, you can help people see the pattern: Monkeys care about social dominance; friends and relatives care about social dominance; and you care about social dominance too.

The person you want to help may refuse to accept the facts. They have always been rewarded for saying, "I don't care about myself; I only care about others." They don't want to lose those rewards. They may bitterly resent the one-down position that they have put themselves in but they cannot see how they are actually creating this dynamic to get rewards.

The person you are trying to help has been shaped by past disappoint-ments, like all of us. You are likely to trigger old pain when you explain the natural urge for social dominance. You will trigger more cortisol if you disrupt their old ways of explaining their frustrations with big monkeys. If they have learned to blame the world for their one-down feelings, they will not appreciate your blaming their circuits.

But you can help by teaching healthy ways to meet our natural need for social importance. When people see a new path to rewards, they stop activating their old reward-seeking habits. You help by focusing on new rewards instead of critiquing old ones. Managing our urge for status is hard, but it's the challenge that comes with the gift of life.

Epilogue

As I finish this book, I am surrounded by conflict over social comparison. People don't understand their strong feelings about social comparison, so they submit to fancy theories pushed by strong social alliances. I have to keep reminding myself that mammals have always bonded around common enemies, and they have always used these bonds to raise their status above rival alliances.

I do not watch the news because it fills your brain with conflict and your body with cortisol. Instead, I learn about the world from other sources.

One of my favorite sources is local museums. When I pass through a small town, I love to stop in the museum. I learned something interesting about group identity while visiting small-town museums in Europe. I saw a lot of traditional costumes, and each region displayed them with great pride. I found this confusing because the costumes looked so similar from one region to another. It was hard to understand why so much pride was invested in such small differences.

I should explain my bias in this matter. I had an international doll collection when I was young, so I saw a variety of folk costumes on my wall every day. It was the era of Disney's *It's A Small World* exhibit, which was symbolized by an array of traditional costumes. When I looked at traditional European garb, the small regional differences did not get my attention.

But they did get the attention of the people who wore them, because people rarely left their village in past centuries. They rarely saw clothing that looked different from their own, so they really noticed small differences in the costume of a neighboring village. They did not think it was a small world.

But why did everyone in the village wear the same garb?

I discovered the answer in a museum of computer history. The Jacquard loom is often called the first computer. Before this loom, fabric patterns were so hard to weave that the average artisan only knew how to create one: the one they learned from their grandparents. Few people had a conceptual knowledge of how to make diverse patterns.

People stuck to what they knew, and in time the local pattern came to symbolize local customs, social bonds, and the feeling of social support. Opportunities to bond outside that group were rare, so it was easy for the brain to associate your fabric pattern with your support network.

Today, our lives are different on the surface, but we have the same basic brain. We repeat patterns learned in youth, and our brains associate publicly visible patterns with private emotional patterns.

The mammal brain is always looking for the best way to be strong. A great example struck me in a local museum on the Oregon Trail. A group of settlers set off on a wagon train to Oregon during the Civil War with some people from the North and some from the South. They all got along while they faced attacks by Native Americans, but as soon as they reached safe territory, they started attacking each other. Fortunately, they realized what they were doing and rebuilt trust.

The mammal brain constantly looks for ways to feel strong and powerful in order to ease its sense of threat. Group bonds help you feel strong, but the good feeling doesn't last because you always see the risk that another group is stronger than yours.

Modern technology gives us the ability to build bigger and bigger groups, but we do not end up feeling stronger and stronger. Instead, we keep comparing our group to some other group, which has also grown larger from modern technology. We end up with the same status games on a larger scale. We apply new technology to the same old quest for the one-up feeling. We end up feeling threatened by every possible risk to our social importance as we define it. If you don't understand your mammal brain, you blame your threatened feelings on others.

Fortunately, each of us has the power to stop status games in our own brain.

Index

About the Author

Loretta Graziano Breuning, PhD, is founder of the Inner Mammal Institute and author of *Habits of a Happy Brain: Retrain Your Brain to Boost Your Serotonin, Dopamine, Oxytocin, and Endorphin Levels.* She's professor emerita of management at California State University, East Bay. Her many books and digital resources help people find their power to manage their brain chemicals. Her work has been translated into many languages and she's frequently heard on podcasts and webinars. Loretta wants to help everyone make peace with their inner mammal.

Dr. Breuning has served as a volunteer for the United Nations in Africa, and as a docent at the Oakland Zoo. She's a graduate of Cornell University and Tufts. In her free time, she travels, watches foreign-language videos, and spends time with her grandchildren.

The Inner Mammal Institute is full of free resources to learn about the brain chemistry we've inherited from earlier mammals (https://innermammalinstitute.org).